SALLY BAYLEY is a writer and lectur[...] College, Oxford. She also teaches on t[...] programme at Wadham College, Oxfor[...] *with Dove* and *No Boys Play Here.* The [...] child-narrator from the previous two books complete her j[...], from reader to writer, is the third part of the trilogy. Sally also hosts and performs the acclaimed immersive podcast, *A Reading Life, A Writing Life*, which offers innovative forms of storytelling, set to music and soundscapes, for a world in crisis.

Praise for **THE GREEN LADY**

'A beguiling, experimental mixture of biography, fiction and family history . . . The prose is glancing and poetic, suffused with gentle melancholy, yet bursting with connections that anticipate, tease and delight . . . There is much here of art and literature as succour for the soul, and this charming, original and poignant book shines with intellectual and imaginative fire'　　　　　　　　　　　**Spectator**

'With each new book, Sally Bayley seems to invent a new literary genre. *The Green Lady* is another bulletin from her unique imagination – a marvel of formal originality and verbal ingenuity. There is no other writer remotely like her'

MATT ROWLAND HILL, author of *Original Sins*

'In a beguiling blend of memoir and storytelling, the author of *Girl with Dove* and *No Boys Play Here* explores the relationship between children and their teachers, and the sustaining power of literature, especially for those growing up in poverty or dealing with neglect and abuse. In search of a better plot, Bayley's protagonist seeks out her maternal ancestors, and other women in history who have paved a path to independence, happiness and artistic freedom in a space of one's own. No one writes quite like Bayley – she's a true, precious original'　　　　　　　　**CAROLINE SANDERSON, *The Bookseller***

Also by Sally Bayley

No Boys Play Here

Girl with Dove

Eye Rhymes: Sylvia Plath's Art of the Visual
(with Kathleen Connors)

Home on the Horizon:
America's Search for Space, from Emily Dickinson to Bob Dylan

Representing Sylvia Plath
(editor, with Tracy Brain)

The Private Life of the Diary: From Pepys to Tweets

SALLY BAYLEY

THE GREEN LADY

A Spirit, A Story, A Place

WILLIAM
COLLINS

William Collins
An imprint of HarperCollins*Publishers*
1 London Bridge Street
London SE1 9GF
WilliamCollinsBooks.com

HarperCollins*Publishers*
Macken House
39/40 Mayor Street Upper
Dublin 1
D01 C9W8 Ireland

First published in Great Britain in 2023 by William Collins
This William Collins paperback edition published in 2024

1

Copyright © Sally Bayley 2023
Illustrations © Anne Griffiths

Sally Bayley asserts the moral right to be identified as the author of
this work in accordance with the Copyright, Designs and Patents Act 1988

A catalogue record for this book is available from the British Library

ISBN 978-0-00-841421-4

Printed and bound in the UK using 100% renewable electricity at CPI Group (UK) Ltd

This book is produced from independently certified FSC™ paper
to ensure responsible forest management

For more information visit: www.harpercollins.co.uk/green

For my grandmother, Edna May Turner,
who taught me that the prickly cactus plant
must be nurtured too, for her rose will come
in the dead of winter.

And by came an angel who had a bright key,
And he open'd the coffins and set them all free.

'The Chimney-Sweeper', from William Blake,
Songs of Innocence and Experience with Other Poems (1866)

1310

PRICE
3/6

SIZE 10
BUST 34

Contents

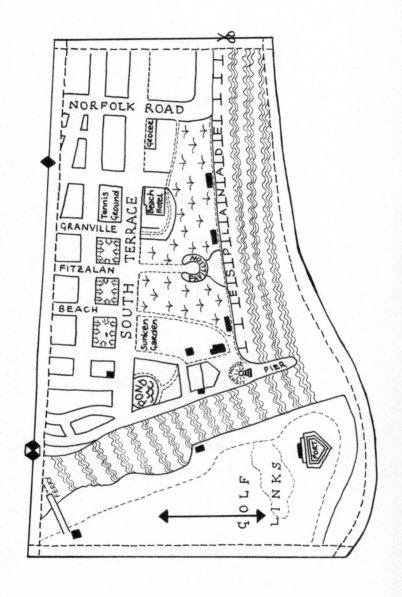

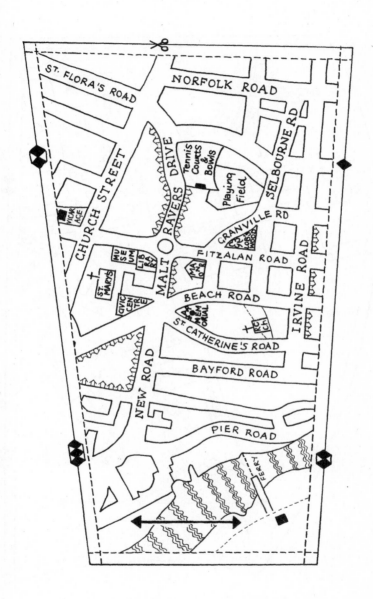

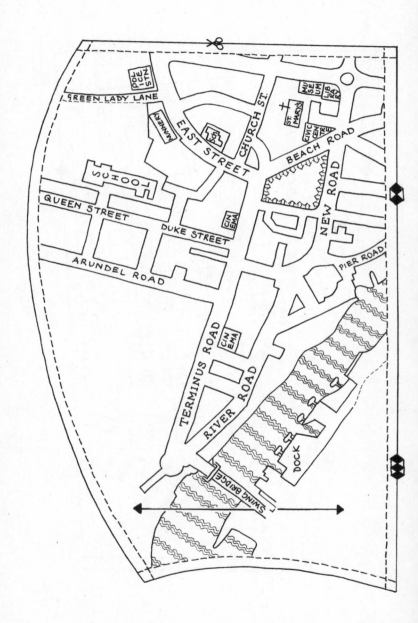

History is full of mothers who lie in bed fretting and forgetting to put out the supper. And so, the Green Lady comes to air the beds, to teach the children to dance and sing. She knows the best bedtime stories and can intuit any kind of folly or danger. She is a kindly ghost, a sensitive visitor, the nanny, the au pair, the home help. You will never see her come; you will never see her go. In Celtic mythology she is a guardian spirit who protects the castle when the family is gone. She is a muse, a spirit of place; she treads delicately and lightly, and never usurps. She is a woman with a heart full of children. When she disappears, the trees whisper – *See, the Green Lady has passed over* – and so her mound begins to grow. *Oh, how we mourn her.* She is life and death and everything in between.

PART ONE

The Sketchbook

PART ONE

The Sketchbook

Nobody knows much about my grandmother Maze, only that she liked dancing and knew the steps to the Charleston and the foxtrot, and as a girl danced upon Shoreham Sands. On Shoreham Sands the wind whipped up and blew her skirt inside out, while Edna May, who we call Maze, was practising dancing with a man called Cyril. And Gladys was there, and she was a ninny and screamed at any little thing; and the wind blew up their skirts and turned them inside out, and Gladys screamed and giggled, screamed and giggled. *Gladys! Gladys! Come back!* In the photograph Maze keeps inside her purse, Gladys is grinning. Gladys is always grinning, and when she rushes out towards the waves, her sister calls her back. *Gladys, Gladys, come back!* And Gladys turns and waves.

My grandmother was born upon saltwater. In the nineteenth century, Shoreham was a picturesque harbour, pretty enough for the famous artist Joseph Mallord William Turner to paint it several times. It's his painting we had pinned up at school, and the one Miss Braithwaite, who liked fetching landscapes, made us practise drawing because teachers want you to see what they see so you can imitate.

No fuss, no frills. Think of Joseph Mallord William Turner . . . the Master.

Masters are no fun, we want to draw people, a picture's no fun without people. HAROLD, NORMAN, CYRIL, EDNA, ELSIE, GLADYS, PHYLLIS, FLORENCE, MAY and MARY. These are the people I see, the old-fashioned people; and they sit on top of the cliff in the painting by Joseph William Turner, having a picnic. And the painter on the seashore looks up and thinks, What a nice shape they make all huddled there together, mouths chattering one to the dozen. But he doesn't concern himself with that – their mouths, their fingers, their chapped red hands, the flapping hems of their skirts, the flying ties on their bonnets or hats – these are washerwomen and it is their one day off. He isn't concerned with any of that this fine day, only with outlines: contours, dips and falls, then rises, the sloping of the cliff, the shape of the cloud hovering above looking blankly on, because she is alone – one sole cloud in the sky – the painter wishes for more.

He looks down, towards the cliffs.

There are the small outlines of these women against the cliff face, their bobbing hats, their bonnets, their noses and faces, a tiny happenstance, an hour or two one Sunday after-noon in 1826 or so, a long time ago. A bubble of laughter, a few fretful words, two women who scold and scorn as they sit drying sheets across their legs, picking barnacles from their skirts.

He looks up towards the cliffs.

It is the cliffs he wants; the sun, the sky, the big blue bay stretching out towards the sea. Gigantic things: the sky running out of light – the sea running out of blue, the sun running out of yellow, turning white, everything turning into light.

I shall paint that, he says, as he pulls his hat off his head, while we scratch and scribble over the bay with our chubby pastel crayons, left to right, right to left, left to right, blue on white on yellow – until we have blocked out the painter's light, and filled the rockpools with brown and scratched over the sand with our scratchy green as we go looking for crabs. But where are the people?

Joseph Mallord William Turner, the famous painter, can make people magically appear behind the clouds; and so, now my grandmother is there, stepping over the sharp rocks. *Mind where you put your feet, Edna, Edna May, be careful! The rocks will tear your stockings! Take them off, you ninny!* I can see Edna May, but Mr Turner does not, he sees only the light.

And William Turner peers until he sees the something coming through the bouncing light – it is soft and forgiving, it blurs things – the ripple of the sails, the billowing waves. *Nothing is still, everything is turning,* he murmurs. *The light turns through the air, and so I must go there.*

So every day the painter comes down from his lodgings near the church which the locals call St Mary de Haura, and he observes the square tower floating above the transept, its crenellations cutting small squares into the blue sky. *I shall draw that shape,* he says to himself. *I shall paint that little church in front of me, which is not so little really; it is quite grand. I will make a sketch and remember the rest.* And Mr William Turner takes out his sketchbook and begins to scratch out the outlines of the church: that oblong, that square, those delicate feathery windows letting in the light. Upwards goes his pencil, up up, and down, moving so fast, airborne his hand. Flutter, flutter, feather, land, but never still for more than a moment. It moves so quickly, the hand of a painter, the eye of an artist. Train your eye to see, *to see*, his teacher said. *Follow the lines, Joseph, where are they going? Where can they go? Ask yourself always: where is the light on the wall?*

It is behind you.

And the people of the town come to look at the painter standing in the graveyard of their little church with his black tricorne hat on and they peer over his shoulder.

They are behind you.

What is he doing standing and peering so hard? What is he looking at, they ask, staring and staring at their flint tower, craning his neck?

They look at the sky: there are only clouds passing over. They look back at the artist, whose hat is bobbing up and down.

He looks at them; he looks up; he looks down.

Hello, good people of Shoreham! I must go down to the estuary now before the light fades, and Mr Turner tips his hat at the polite mouths and stares.

They watch him go, his mouth still moving.

Mr Joseph Turner is murmuring.

It is the light that I want, yellow turning to white, white turning to sea blue and back to white, across the waves. See how it spreads! It is turning like a Catherine wheel, faster and faster. See how it burns!

The painter murmurs.

Now, let's move towards the pale blue sea, the light is kinder there; the colour of bluebells floating on water, blanching as they wash over the rocks. And there is a girl stepping gingerly in between, her boots tied around her neck, her stockings wrapped around her waist.

She is faltering.

Her feet are aching.

But Joseph Turner will not paint her because he cannot see her coming through the light – it blinds him – and it will be another nine decades before she reaches those rocks.

Over the years it will fade and fall; your house of delicate lines will crumble. What you did not structure carefully will slough off and fall into the sea. A granite pencil can only preserve a faint smile. Joseph Mallord William Turner knew to carry three or four on his person. Memory work is treacherous. History is the same. And what you once recalled may now stand against you. So preserve your lines, grip your pencil, and press down hard. Restore those faint lines. Observe the chalk's gradient, from puckered sky to sandy wrinkles.

the colour of bluebells
floating on water

How far the cliff line stoops before it needs recovering. Before your hands are turned stiff and cold from trying to catch the contour on the horizon. That is the church, half a mile from here, she has a Saxon tower.

The artist opens his notebook, his hands all a-flurry. Like Patience he sits upon his monument, smiling at grief – see, the sun has been setting for a while, and soon she will fade – but the goddess Mnemosyne is cruel and rarely smiles back. She will only take, never receive, so you had better write it down, all you can remember. Billowing shapes and outlines, the solid matter beneath your feet. What you take to be the present, what you make of the past, can only be known away from here. Mr Joseph Mallord William Turner slips over the rocks and wishes his feet were steadier; the soles of his shoes are wearing through; his attitude is thinning. He is a gruff man.

And memory is a fragile creature. Out at sea she will never save you; her thread is too bare, her petticoats spare. You must tie your own knots, make your own nets, repair, and repair. The painter scrunches his eyes, the light is dimming, he does not have long to know this place. His heart flutters, his hands dance and jig. At sunset, the painter opens his vermilion wings.

If only he had pressed harder, we might have seen more, but Joseph Mallord William Turner is a sensitive man and his wrists tread lightly. Granite on paper. Pieces of flinty rock, the stem of his pencil dislodging, flying over the paper, a gull. Rapid, rapid, the movement of his eyes. An artist is a nonchalant creature who sees only what he wants. So much yawning space in between. That could be you, that could be me, but we are ignored; he does not want us here. Memory work is divination, a hard press down upon the hands of fate. And the artist is a solitary creature, he does not want to paint us. But we are here, we look on, the people.

Here is the church, here is the steeple, here are the raggedy people. The women who sit and do their work. Thread, and thread like Penelope, weaving together their talk. What you can't see you hear. The writer knows that, and so she listens for the thick dip of his Cockney voice, musty and strong. *That strain again, it had a dying fall.* Joseph Mallord William Turner, born over a barber's shop, slips down from the harbour wall. A diminutive man, small and squat, but he can recall a sharp line, the length of the harbour wall, the steady tread of mortar.

'Ivy white,' said Miss Braithwaite. 'He drew on ivy white. His lines were faint, but he was a great master.'

Disappearing, always disappearing, said the painter, 'into the light'.

Distant Lines

My grandmother, Edna May Turner, a distant relative of the famous painter, was born into a line of men who lived above shops. Small men with grand dreams counting pennies at the end of the day. First came Cyril. I remember that, and the sound of his name, like sweet syrup running through teeth. *Cyril*, whistling on the wind. I said it again and again. Cyril, who always sounded naughty.

Grand uncle Cyril, who was far away now but had once been lying out in the garden with his sister in Shoreham-by-Sea, a stone's throw from the church. Cyril, who one day would be an ironmonger and have his own shop with copper pots and pans. That little shop on the corner, opposite the church on West Street – that's Cyril's. He liked the sound of clanging pots; he liked the sound of money and no one to shout over him. Uncle Cyril, I only know what your sister said of you and sisters are never reliable. So I will console you, I will tell you stories, because in the end we only have tales to tell, and behind every story is another story, those old ghosts waving their arms. We live among ghosts. Uncle Cyril, I lived with you for years, and your name was as faint as the cumulus clouds I lie under now trying to summon your shape. I know you liked pans, because your sister does too, coppery and shiny and never to be burned. But your pans would be displayed differently, not all in the window, not as your father did. Like father, like son, but not the same, never the same. Cyril says he will display his pans differently. *Further up and further in.* Who said that? A man before your time, Cyril, long before your time.

Edna May's folk were tailors sprung from the shops on Savile Row. My great-grandfather was a tailor and sat cross-legged in a row with other tailors sewing and sewing until his joints began to ache and he got the cramp. *The cramp, I've got the cramp,* he said, although there was no time to do anything about it, because soon enough the sky would begin to turn pink and blue, which is the time of tailoring on Savile Row. The early hours of the morning when no one in their right mind is up yet – but the tailors are – sitting cross-legged with a silk garment spread over their knees humming the threading and thumbing their way into dawn.

Their work, their early morning work, such fine stitching and threading, such delicate weaving of soft fabric to fabric and lining to yielding lining. And the tailor knows – only he knows – that the buttonholes are delicate flowers spreading open to greet that stern metal thing that would poke their eyes out. Brass buttons, sometimes silver, occasionally gold; these are gold, because this is royal livery, and these buttons are of the finest quality, gold tipped, gold dipped. Tiny gold spheres glittering in the sun.

They wink and cheer for him soon to be king, the portly man

who loves his waistcoats and jackets. Requiring such fine work – those little buttonholes, those tiny stitches darting back and forth – as quick as the sun across the estuary, wink, wink, and it's gone. They throw the light too, those little discs, flirting with the next lady who comes their way at the Windsor Spring Ball. There is one every year, and Bertie must have a new jacket to swing his way across the ballroom floor. And so, the work must be done to those little buttons – what craftsmanship, so well regarded, from Shoreditch to Somers Town, from Bermondsey to Brompton Market – they all know of *Mr Henry Bayley at your service!* A little mouse who sat up all night until he lost half his sight, stitching together suit patterns and high shoulders, and two buttons on the waist to draw in that grin.

Men like to look slender, and it helps if you're tall. How tall was the Prince of Wales when he ordered his dinner jacket: one with pockets and smart enough to turn a prince into a king? Edward VII who turned king for nine years. From 1901 to 1910, three years before my grandmother was born, this plump prince, who everyone called Bertie, was responsible for ordering a special blue silk jacket, short, ending midway down the thighs, with two gold buttons at the front.

All that beer and wine swilling around on nights out on the town *with some silly wench*, said the old queen to her son. Victoria, on her last pegs, and furious at Bertie for having it off with a woman called Nellie on the side of a cliff somewhere. Nellie, ripping his new suit from left to right until his belly hung out. The suit had to be made again, it was unsalvageable, and Mr Poole of Savile Row who owned the shop where my great-grandfather worked was not happy with the crown prince when he saw the mess he had made of his beautiful work, and he ordered his set of six tailors to stay up all night to mend the torn silk jacket.

And so, my great-grandfather was called in from his sleepy bed, and the gas lamps were lit, and they stayed lit until a new blue smoking jacket had been drawn up on paper. And stitches run along the breast and shoulders and down the back, allowing a little more room, a bit more width, and across the front too – the breast again, look at those lovely lapels, smooth as silk, no satin, or girls' sashes – and then the waist, add another two inches there.

'Where is my tailor?' said the prince.

'Henry Bayley at your service!'

A renowned tailor and my ancestor who sat cross-legged all night on a trestle table, and when the morning light came up, he stood to stretch his back and legs and peer out the window. Then went to fetch himself a draught of cold water and set the kettle on the stove. Mr H. Bayley, firm-thumbed and -fingered, calluses on all five, and hard skin across the top of his palms, stares out the window again and closes his eyes. Tiredness running down them like a bank of dry sand, and so Henry Bayley keeps his eyes shut for as long as he can. Not long though, not long. He only has until teatime.

The prince is coming at five o'clock to fetch his new jacket.

But how can he expect it to be the same as the last? Princes grow. We never mention it of course; just add an inch or two and pretend everything is the same.

Henry Bayley opened his eyes and poured out his tea.

The Great Storm

Mr HENRY BAYLEY peering from his narrow window at dawn scrunches up his eyes. He is tired. Soon his eyes will be failing him. My grandmother's eyes are tired too from all that watching. Edna May Turner was always watching; from the window two floors above, from her kitchen hovel. So many children to watch over now the wind was getting up; so many falling trees.

Ghost stories often begin with the wind getting up, the wind shrieking through windows. Wind, windows, rattling cords, curtains whipped back like hair. I remember Jane Eyre whose story began with a wintry wind and a child peering through a window. 'There was no possibility of taking a walk that day,' Jane said to herself, as my grandmother said to me when she peered from the kitchen window. 'The wind is getting up. *Have next door noticed yet? He's out with his spade, and she's supervising. Does he know the wind is picking up? Can he see?*' What can any of us see now the clouds have passed over, now the leaves have begun to spin, the branches to fall?

Only the chestnut tree at the back of the house leaning and stretching, her old roots aching. Tree dragged by the hair between Mrs Sturgess's wall and ours. She is old, she is tired, she has seen too much. Now she is rotting at the roots; the rats and foxes have eaten her; they have done their worst, hidden dark things. Tree is ready to fall, her time has come. The old witch is falling, but we don't want her dead – we've watched her for years – she was our ayah, our nanny, our nurse. Behind Tree there is another story of a little girl left all alone: an orphan-child, a dead mother. The night of the great storm I had a dream; I dreamed of a girl called Mary.

History is full of unwanted children. There is Mary Lennox in *The Secret Garden*. Mary's mother is dead, Mary's father is dead, and so Mary lies alone in her room pulling the covers up over her head. Her mother's face floats towards her. Mother wears a lace collar; she sips a pink, frothy drink; she is smiling and laughing. Men in uniform are gathered around her, their mouths wide and hungry. Mary can see their teeth – she leans in – but a loud noise startles her. Glass breaks and shatters, a gust of wind blows in, the bungalow shakes. At the back of the house there are muffled cries.

Mary sleeps, later she wakes. She's hungry, a fox, a ferret, a wild cat. She creeps out from behind her bedroom door. Everything is still, nothing moves; but no, something stirs in the corner? It is a mouse scampering beneath the chairs. Mary climbs onto a chair and pulls at the tablecloth. She reaches towards the plate: some biscuits, a triangle of cheese, a glass half full, filled with something sweet and red – Mary drinks – it is strong. She carries the plate back to her room, the door creaks. She eats and drinks and falls asleep. When she wakes up, everyone is gone. There's only an old snake slipping under her door; he has jewelled eyes; she thinks of her mother.

Her mother was pretty, they said, the people who found her. She was very pretty and wore lace, but she had not been well. *She has a high fever, Mary!* Something purple got into her veins, they call it *cholera*. And now the ayah has run away; the dark-haired girl has run back to her family in the hills. 'It is too late, too late . . . too late!' Mary can hear the yells. Someone has left something too late, and her ayah has run away. There are screams in the night, the hurrying sound of feet, I wake. Someone has died, there is panic and confusion, there is wailing in the night, mysterious and frightening sounds. It is the trees, they are screaming, they want to take back the land. To raze the flats opposite, to dismantle the cladding made from such cheap materials. Wilder and wilder the trees wail, wilder and wilder my grandmother's voice. 'Everyone cutting corners, the council using flimsy bits of prefabricated this and that' – it all blew away the night of the great storm – every bit of it.

They said it wasn't a hurricane because it didn't start in the tropics, but the winds were stronger than any wind seen for hundreds of years, so they call it the Great Storm. Just along the coast boats were turned over, and somewhere a man in a farmhouse was killed. His name was Cyril, though the weatherman swore blind it wasn't coming, but she came, and she battered the coast something dreadful. We didn't go to school that day. The town roads were blocked, nothing could get through, so we sat and peered out the window and wondered how much of it we had heard at night and how much we had missed. My grandmother turned on the radio for the news report.

The flats along Sea Road have taken a terrible battering; the cladding has blown off, curled up and ripped away, torn into the sea, so the man on the radio told my grandmother, who told us – all across the airwaves the sounds of distress. Eighteen people killed that night, that morning, most of them along the coast, but one or two inland: that poor bugger in the farmhouse – the bricks fell in and he suffocated – all that chalk and rubble over his face.

The windows in the arcade were smashed, the nave windows at St Michael's too; and the old elm tree at the back has fallen right across the churchyard. Think of the fire brigade next door; all sorts of work for them to do now, hauling up those trees.

And the elms along the main road, near the golf course, do they still stand? Dark figures standing starkly, their trunks are like vases, proud survivors of Dutch elm disease. Dark-green leaves turned brown. Beetles ate through the bark carrying deadly fungus, and now the leaves are dead and shrivelled. People don't realise, but all around them stand dead and dying trees.

All this the man on the radio must know. He reports on the place where I live, the town, the road leading out to the Downs, the windy A259 towards Worthing, probably closed now after the storm. His voice travels across the land, from the sea to the hills to the trees on top. On Highdown the trees are still standing: the old oaks, the supple beeches, the wych elms. People take their relatives up there on Sundays for a bit of a blow around – the wind in your hair, that's how you like it, isn't it? He bends down to touch my grandmother's hair. The man on the radio is following us. His voice travels everywhere.

My grandmother was born on gusts of wind, and the strongest gusts recorded that night were in Shoreham-by-Sea. Waves came up over the sea wall, and cars were soaked to the skin; a fisherman was blown against a beach hut and killed. 115 mph recorded on Shoreham seafront. A man called Mr Keen coordinated the recovery effort. He asked the people of Shoreham and further afield, Lancing and Sompting, Worthing, and up into the Downs towards Horsham and Haywards Heath, to tie ribbons and rags around the limbs of dangerous trees. Condemned beeches and conifers, precarious firs, trees damned to die whether they'd been uprooted or not. The beech trees on Chanctonbury Ring have gone, planted in 1760; now the hill's stark naked, stripped of cover, *how terribly sad*, said Mr Keen, first name Frank. The bishop's wall around the palace in Chichester has been smashed through by an enormous oak. The town of Sevenoaks has lost six of its trees, leaving only one. All this we must know.

So Frank went on the radio and addressed the people of Sussex. They should tie rags and ribbons around any dangerous tree; the council would come and uproot it and take it away;

or the army. Fifty Gurkhas drafted in from Aldershot to clear up the mess bringing lorries and tanks, was it? Mr Keen wasn't quite sure. Better not put that out on the radio, you don't want to alarm people.

A hundred and fifteen miles per hour, the man on the radio said, the newsman and his team. Keen to get the word out. Keen to spread the news, but is it *good*? My grandmother is listening in. She's turning the dial up; she is pulling out the antenna; she is leaning into the speaker – where is it? The voice of the man speaking to her, where has he gone? Now it's the weather and the weatherman is on, but it's not the man who got it all wrong, surely? Mr Fish, *what was he thinking*? Hadn't he been out on the waters, tested the tide, felt the current? This one came from the Bay of Biscay; she collided with some very cold currents. Mr Fish should know this. There were men lost at sea that night, and a man called Cyril was lying in bed when the legs of his bed were forced through the ceiling below. The entire roof of his house fell down and Cyril was covered in rubble. His brother was on his way with a chainsaw, but he got there too late. By the time he arrived the chimney had fallen in.

Chimneys were falling in all over southern England. Chimneys and men like Cyril caught beneath the rubble, looking for their mothers. The old dear had gone to bed, but she was pulled out by neighbours – her room was downstairs – that's what saved her. Sleeping downstairs. The chimney didn't get her, but Cyril suffocated beneath the rubble. No bones broken but he couldn't breathe. Killed by bricks and mortar, killed by dust. Poor Cyril. The cattle will bray for him today. The cows will moan and moo their prayers. If only Cyril had slept downstairs. His brother stood there with a chainsaw but there was nothing to hack into. Outside, the trees lay dead all around, but inside there was only a pile of bricks breathing in the dust.

Cyril and Mrs Plover

I CAN'T STOP THINKING of Cyril, the man we read about in the paper, the man we heard on the news. Maze told me that Cyril had disappeared under a pile of rubble, and it made her think of her brother who was dead and gone, he was Cyril too. Cyril worked on the local farm. At six o'clock he got up to go and feed the cows. There were two stringy ones at the back of the farmhouse he shared with his neighbour. He crossed the field, went through a gate and then another gate, and this one was flimsy and held together by rope. Cyril fed the cows as a matter of habit. It was what he did as a child. He liked the early morning swishing of wet grass around his ankles and the sound of the gate creaking open; the metal hinges sometimes got stuck so he took out his oil can and added a few drops. Just a little drop goes a long way. Cyril keeps the oil can in his pocket. He wears his old blue overalls in the morning and his wellington boots. Mrs Plover next door has a soft spot for Cyril. She has him in for tea.

'It must be hard for you with your mother, Cyril,' she says to him. 'It can't be easy for a young man like you all by yourself.'

'I'm not so young, ma'am,' says Cyril shyly. 'I'm older than the old beak looks.' Mrs Plover thought that must be some sort of country saying. Cyril had a quaint way with words. She liked listening to him speak. Mrs Plover's husband, Harold, had been dead a few years. A nasty accident. She didn't like to speak of it, at least not right away. *Not now, Hilda, not now, put it away!*

'Cyril, come and make yourself at home.'

Cyril sat down by the window and looked out.

'Now let's have some tea,' and she begins to hum a tune. '"All Things Bright and Beautiful", Harold, that's my favourite.' She sometimes called him that.

'Yes, ma'am.'

'Hilda, Cyril. We've known each other long enough now.'

'Yes, ma'am.'

'The old hymns are best, Cyril.'

'Yes, ma'am.'

'What hymns do you like, Cyril?'

'Don't know as I know many, ma'am.'

'Everyone knows a hymn or two, Cyril . . . from school.'

'Don't have a good memory for words, ma'am.'

'"All Things Bright and Beautiful" is so *cheering*, Cyril.'

Cyril liked Mrs Plover, but she sometimes made him feel uncomfortable; she looked at him in a peculiar way. One day she offered to polish his shoes and Cyril could feel himself blushing. Pink was uncomfortable, so was red. As a child he'd had chilblains from walking through the wet fields. He hadn't noticed his toes turning pink until at night when they began to bother him. Hot as pokers.

'Went to bed wi' your socks on, I suppose!' His mother presumed he knew and that everyone knew, you don't let your socks dry out on your feet. But he'd forgotten. Cyril was always forgetting things. But he never forgot when harvest time was, or when it was the first chicks might be seen in the hen coop, or when the moorhen babies might appear on the river – he knows all the routes around Amberley and Bury – he walks for miles does Cyril.

Cyril lives in Wick, which isn't a very grand place; it's far from grand. Wick is a muddy place. You can sink low here. Cyril grew up on a farm. He was raised among cows. There's nothing he likes more than the sound of cows mooing. They calm him; cows are calm, it's just a fact.

Cows gather in the fields behind the old laundry. They used to call it a steam house. Cyril was sent there with bundles of sheets on Saturday mornings. These were from the lodger's room, and his mother sent him when she didn't have time to get things done herself. She knew one of the girls who worked at the laundry and lived in a cottage nearby. It was a treat to have the bedding done by someone else, but Cyril hated carrying those old sheets around, it was girl's work. He ran as fast as he could to the steam house, an ugly old place he thought, for he couldn't see its beauty, its peculiar beauty, of bricks and mortar funnelling up towards tall, elegant chimneys. Cyril was no artist, he was no architect, he took no notice of inanimate things. Swishing tails, he preferred those. He hated the steam laundry; she was a saggy old dragon, where cross women with pink cheeks yelled and turned mangles.

It only happened once or twice, as a treat, his ma said, but Cyril remembers it like it was every week on wash day. His mother, lying in the downstairs room, would tell you it was only once or twice; because she knew Rose Ferrars who worked at the laundry, and Rose let her sneak in some sheets just for a treat, pretending they were Mrs Forsyth's from the manor up Lyminster way. Children don't know any of this, who does what for whom by way of a treat or a favour. They know only the stories they are told that adults tell themselves as a way of reconciling one thing with another. The facts, the fiction, but there are always a few facts left in the purse, a bit of old change rattling about. The facts: that Cyril's mother, Mrs Homewood, had told herself before she told Rose at the laundry before Rose knew anything about it. Before Cyril was commissioned to carry the sheets to Rose by way of Dark Alley, the twitten running down past the public house where ghosts gather to jump on poor souls wandering by. Cyril shuddered when he went underneath the mulberry tree, its dark red fruit lying splat upon the ground. Red fists, red faces, Cyril saw them all coming through the dark.

'Nothing like it used to be,' sighs Mrs Plover, cradling her mug of tea. Hilda Plover lives off Lyminster Way, near the Knucker Hole where once a man called Jim Puttock slew the watery dragon in his dark pit. That was a long time ago. You can find her house if you steer off the main road. Best not take a car, they say, not down those narrow lanes. Better to walk. The lane is covered in grass and stones and there are cattle grids, so watch your step. 'Mind how you go, Harold,' Hilda always said. Women say that a lot, as though the mind moves of its own accord, and it does; the body follows behind. Harold had no idea where he was going when first he began to tread beneath the damp soil, only that he lies six feet under, while Hilda tramples on overhead.

*

We eat stories as cows eat fodder. 'Did you know about the story of the Knucker, Cyril? Did they teach you that at school?' Mrs Plover asked one afternoon; she liked to tell stories. She sometimes read to children at the local school. 'When they'll have me, Cyril. They won't want an old thing like me around much longer.' Mrs Plover took a good look at him.

'What did they teach you at school, Cyril?'

'They didn't tell us nothing interesting, Mrs Plover.'

'Hilda, Cyril.'

'I remember some silly talk about some monster.'

'Oh, the Knucker isn't silly talk, Cyril. That's history that is. The Knucker is a dragon who lives in a hole . . .' Cyril scratched his head. Mrs Plover didn't half have some funny ideas. 'Let me tell you about the Knucker, Cyril.' He shifted in his chair. Stories took a while.

The Knucker is a water dragon and lives inside dark holes. You might say inside wells, you might say muddy ditches, but they prefer something more concealed. Knuckers don't like to be too exposed, so they come out at night, like bats, and they appear in old poetry.

On then went the atheling-born
o'er stone-cliffs steep and strait defiles,
narrow passes and unknown ways,
headlands sheer, and the haunts of the Nicors.

A Nicor is a *Knucker*, which is a water dragon. An atheling is someone royal. A nobleman. A brave man. A man who walks alone for days, for months, with fierce valour in his heart and his sword thrust forward. Cyril's brother, Alec, was a man with valour in his heart, and the night of the Great Storm he struck out for the farm, the Homewood's, that old place with three tall brick chimneys reaching for the sky. And Alec passed through known ways now made unknown by all those felled trees; and his passes were narrow, for the trees did not let him through that night; no, they barred his way, on the early morning of 16 October 1987. How old were you? Older than I remember. We are all older than we remember, but once Cyril was a child clinging to slippery boughs; and high upon the tractor and the haycart piling up the yellow stuff. Scarecrow's hair, he called it, like the other folk. Because children imitate, and children make the sounds that adults make. And Cyril, who knew how to moo like a cow, has joined the moss-covered folk.

Down the Green Lady

'There would be a new ayah and perhaps she would
know some new stories.'

WE EAT STORIES as cows eat fodder. Hilda Plover knew that,
and Maze too, who told me of a lady who lived down the Green
Lady. Her name was Mary Neal and she lived in the big house
on the corner. The one we were always trying to see into but
couldn't, because the curtains were drawn, and the windows
were dark and chimney dust flew off the roof. 'A hostel,' said
Maze, 'just for the summer months. They keep it shut up the rest
of the time.' A white house on the corner of the lane. A white
house with shutters. I looked for Mary's face, but the shutters
never opened, Mary's face is blank, but once the shutters were
open and Mary was speaking.

'I want to live among the poor,' Mary said to her mother.
'I want to live among the working people.'

'What a peculiar thing to say,' Mother said. 'You really are a
most peculiar child. You'll do no such thing. Poor people should
stay where they are.'

And you are a very silly woman, thought Mary, I shall not do
as you say!

It all began the day she found a young chimney sweep stuck inside the coal hole with 'an 'orrible stomach ache. Nuffin' to eat since yesterday.' So Mary went to Cook and bought back some apple tart and the boy sat on the edge of the coal hole and ate the tart faster than anyone she'd ever seen eat anything. So she went back for more.

Then Mary asked Mother, 'Why are we all so fat, why is Grandfather fat, why are we always eating?' And Mother hissed at her, 'Wash out your mouth!'

Mary, Mary, quite contrary – my mother called me that too – but now I see Mary's face peeking from the window, and it is like my grandmother's face, yet once Mary was young. She wore a pinafore dress tied behind her back with a sash bow and a petulant look. Mary is cross, Mary is young, Mary is old, that's history. One day you wake up and you look at yourself in the mirror and you see an old lady with a crinkly face while the child is still peeking out. My grandmother's eyes were soft and small and sometimes red with weeping, but it's her hands that I recall most of all. Blue and papery thin, blue rivers on white sand with peppery ridges.

What do you do if you don't have photographs: if they're lost and blown away? You build a new house with apertures and frames; you open the doors and windows and let yourself in; because a photograph is only one way of seeing, and mine have all blown away. The light is good down the Green Lady – go there – the pictures will be strong, and you will see my grandmother coming through the light. Her hands, papery white and blue, turning red from the wind; the dented wire fence we pushed through; the bumpy lane uncovered like a farmer's track, pale and balding; and the farmer, a bald man scratching his pate. I learned that word and wrote it down; it is an old word. William Shakespeare. I put it in my purse. Always there are words you carry, and it was my grandmother who taught me how to read. I stole words from her purse, and I rode away. And the people of the town say:

> Always with her grandmother as a child,
> with her grandmother, never with her mother.
> With: *to carry along, to accompany, to live alongside,*
> *Someone without whom you could not live.*
> *Your succour, your nurture, your roots,*
> *the one who causes you to grow:*
> *who first taught you words.*
> *After she died you saw her everywhere*
> *with you, without you, underground.*
> *And what can you see of her now*
> *with this big green hedge in the way?*
>   *Where is the lady with the child's smile?*
> *Something is in the way.*

Still, I hear my grandmother speak. *Now mount up! Mount* was my grandmother's word. You mounted a horse, you mounted a bicycle, you mounted the Downs around our town; then turned around and looked back at this place, your town, these people, those who had raised you. *Mount:* to get up on a horse; *mounter:* to ascend a mountain; a medieval word: to rise up, to ascend, to fly; from old French *monter,* to go up, to climb; from Latin *montare,* mountain. If you look up the roots of words you can mount higher and higher, or go lower and lower, depending on how you use them. Use them wisely, Maze said, words can turn against you. By the time I was eight, I had too many pictures inside my head, from all the stories I'd been told, and all the ghosts I'd seen. I had to put them somewhere, so I sent them all down the Green Lady. I mounted my grandmother's bicycle and went down the lane every day for months, for years, until I was old enough to take myself to school; until I had the words. And along the way I counted everything I saw: the wooden fence posts, the bunches of blackberry bushes, the number of berries. 'Ready for picking, you'll have to come back after school with a bowl.' And when we got to the big house on the corner, I counted the number of windows and doors and began to look for Mary Neal, the woman who lives in history.

Mary Neal

THE PEOPLE OF the town still speak of an old lady out front, watering her flowers. They still speak of Mary who was atheling born. Her father owned a button factory in Birmingham in 1860: an old filthy beast of a thing, filled with whirring and piercing and stamping of acorn shells. *Oh what pretty shapes made by such delicate hands*, the ladies of Birmingham town used to say. Small hands, poor hands, turning copper, brass, steel, silk, satin, linen, horn, jet, glass, porcelain and shell to the light. But pearl buttons were the costliest of all and only the old hands were allowed to go near those. Buttons made from oyster shells – see how they glint and gleam and – *oh, Elsie, wouldn't you love to pin one of those to your bosom?*

Shh, the foreman's coming. Put your head down. Back to work. Never be caught with your hands off the workbench.

In any case you won't be heard; it's too loud to speak in the factory.

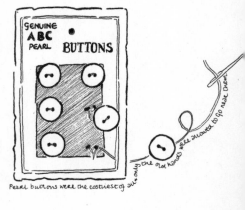

GENUINE
A BC
PEARL BUTTONS

Peael buttons weae the costliest of all only the old hands weee allowed to go neae these

The machines are always whirring, the beast is always working. Poor little things, hear them shriek as they go into the jaws of those steel clamps. Oysters die shrieking and no one will think twice of them again, in the City of Birmingham, or Bromichan (Bromwich-ham) as it was once called, or sometimes rudely, as *Brummagem* which means – 'cheap, bad goods, a poor imitation, not the real thing, tut-tut, *what on earth are they making there?*' – nonetheless *Brummagem* is said to be a well-built and populous town. 'The inhabitants, mostly being smiths, are ingenious in their ways and vend vast quantities of all sorts of iron wares.'

Someone said that and wrote it down as they passed through Bromwichham and saw a town spilling over with men making things from metal and men buying things made from metal-work everywhere.

Merchants with big houses set back from the road, those ingenious artificers of Bromichan, known for its makers of boxes and buckles and buttons, all from iron and steel; and much din there is of hammers and anvils and files, it fair sets your nerves on edge. Jaggedy-jaggedy-jugged-jug are the nerves after a twelve-hour shift, but you get used to it. Now Elsie, take off your pinny so you can walk through this large and populous town, and wend your way home: the upper part of which stands dry on the side of a hill, while the other, lower down, is watery and murky and inhabited by a meaner sort of people. It is these people Mary wished to know, and she'd go down on her hands and knees to know them, she said, because it is God's work to serve those who have less than you: the people who live around the watery ditch, low to the ground.

And so the people speak of Mary. A lady on a penny farthing bicycle followed by her friend. Backs stiff as ramrods – that was the fashion then – to sit outdoors as you did inside, with your spine *straight as a die*. And so, they followed one another at a pretty pace, to the white house on the corner. Mary at the front, head down and pushing forward, into the wind. To her hair clings a bonnet, a small flat pallet of straw tied with a bow beneath her chin. Her jaw juts out slightly and her smile is broad. Look closely: Mary has kind eyes.

'Emmeline! Are you there?'

'I'm here, Mary!'

Always the same patter, always the same rhythm: the clicking of the gate, the wheels turning briskly over the grass, the struggle to lift the bicycle back against the wall: Mary first, then Emmeline. Two friends down for the summer holiday. Two women in a large white house. Emmeline has sketched it once or twice, *for posterity*, she says to her friend, 'because it's nice to have a memory, Mary, of what has been'.

It is 1906 and the house has only been theirs for one summer: two women sitting in the window of the Green Lady Hostel on the corner of the lane. Soon, the girls will arrive from the slums of Somers Town, wan and pale and underfed. The house will restore them, the sea air, the crisp waves, the salt on their skin. Mary has such faith in sea air. Mary has plans, she always has plans. The beds must be clean.

'Emmy, are the beds done?'

'Yes, Mary dear, the girl came this morning.'

'I shall go and air the rooms.'

'Take a moment, Mary. Take a moment and let's sit in the sun.' Always the calm one, Emmeline. Gentle, complete.

'When will Lily come?'

'The day after tomorrow.'

'With the girls.'

'The girls.'

Those girls who sewed all day in the slums of Somers Town. Backs bent over whirring needles that took off their fingers and nails if they weren't careful. Sewing lining into pockets, patches of silk and cotton no one would ever see. They broke their fingers over those; bent their bones double; pricked their skin until it bled. And their backs were weary, and their necks stiff, and in the summer the sun beat down upon them through the large windows, and in the winter the holes in the glass gave them chills. Blood froze in their veins and their feet cramped and their muscles stiff and achy at the end of the day. When one tried to stand, she fell over, and the foreman came and kicked her in the stomach – then someone blew a whistle.

History is full of unwanted children. Take the little chimney sweep Mary found below stairs holding his stomach and crying. He was tired, he was hungry, but only Mary saw him, because no one went below stairs except her, and she came back up covered in soot. Later, Nurse had found her drawing on the nursery wall and there was trouble; what on earth possessed her? Nurse was in no mood for nonsense.

They called her Nurse, not Nanny, because she had been

a nurse once and fitted bandages to soldiers who'd fallen on battlefields. No one could quite remember where, but it wasn't the Battle of Waterloo – Nurse wasn't that old – perhaps the Crimea? Did Nurse go to Russia? No, to Constantinople, and it was so cold that toes and fingers fell off and maggots crawled out – it was hell on earth – but Nurse was terribly brave and stoical. That's why Father liked her. Mother wasn't so sure: Nurse was too confident; she preferred staff to be meek-mannered, small. But Nurse was not a small person; she was a large ball of ammunition. Cannon fodder. She spoke her mind when speaking was required; sometimes a look was enough. She could shoot down an entire regiment with those stony eyes, those pursed lips, that mouth ever so slightly opened.

This morning Mary was in disgrace because she'd soiled the nursery walls with awful black marks. *What on earth possessed you, Mary Neal?* her mother demanded. *You're a disgusting little primitive, that's what you are.* Mary thought this unfair; she'd only wanted to know what it was like to bring soot into the house, to have soot everywhere, all over your hands and toes and clothes. *What chimney sweep?* Mother grimaced. Mother didn't notice people like chimney sweeps. She lifted her hand to her brow. Now what about luncheon? Had Rose changed the flowers? But when she saw Mary streaked with black marks, all over her white pinafore dress and running down her fair hair, she was horrified. *You little beast! Go and wash at once. Ask Nurse to come immediately. What on earth is going on? Are we all turning into savages?*

'I was painting,' said Mary to Nurse when she asked.

'You can't paint with soot.'

'All right, I was drawing then.'

'You'll go and get a pan of water right now and scrub this wall down. You've made a terrible mess. It'll need papering over no doubt. It's filthy in here! Not fit for a dying soldier!'

Why did Nurse always insist on bringing soldiers into everything?

'Your clothes are ruined, so you might as well carry on as you are! Now quick march!'

And Nurse lifted her arms and went storming out of the room. Mary looked at the wall: her drawing. Could no one see that face, that pair of cheeks, those eyes bare and hollow beneath a ragged fringe?

PART TWO

What the Child Saw

I AM HAUNTED BY THE IDEA of becoming old; and I am haunted by old ladies, those who raised me, now forgotten and discarded; and I am haunted by myself because all writers, once they start reporting on life, turn into ghosts. Gasping spirits breathing in good and bad thoughts, fear, wonder and amazement. A writer's notebook is full of the sound of atmosphere; lungs sucking up the air.

I learned this at school: that some people live this life rifling through cabinets and drawers. Take Miss Cull, my music teacher: there she is rummaging through her bag. Miss Cull is always rummaging, poor soul. *What are you looking for, who have you lost?* Deeds, a will, some inheritance. *Fill your notebook, Miss Cull, there are no walls behind you; you're as nameless as a ghost.*

Miss Edith Cull doesn't have a house; she lives in a flat. She doesn't have bolted iron gates with stone lions ready to growl. She is quite confined, restricted, poor Miss Cull needs room to grow.

I pity her.

Pity is a terrible emotion to be stuck with, a dried husk, an acorn shell blown on the wind. Look, there is no nut inside: the squirrel has been, and eaten, and poor Miss Cull is covered in leftover husks. They cleave to her; they ruin her clothes. Now she is shuffling through her bag again, she is looking for her music, her bass cleff, her notes. 'All Things Bright and Beautiful' in the key of G for God. In another life she would choose the same hymn. Miss Cull is a reliable sort; *I will keep her.*

Writers are haunted, which is why we keep notebooks; to store up our ghosts, to let them dance and sing. Writers collect ghosts: return to the same old spots, leave gifts and flowers, say prayers to their relics. Writers are haunted; look at our dreams; this is where it all begins, the second life. Write down your dreams, I say, they will tell you what you are missing. The woman, the girl.

It is always the same dream. I'm on a train and the country-side around is passing by. But it is very blurry, and I can't distinguish anything in particular – no landmarks, no specific attributes, no hills or trees – but I know the landscape is passing me by because that is what happens on trains. Nothing else is going on and I'm alone in my carriage; there are no fellow passengers and I have no ticket, but we are moving. I have no idea where I am going, only that we are heading somewhere, the train and me. I look ahead and there is the blank wall of the carriage. I keep staring and nothing happens, but the train keeps moving smoothly along. I know I'm not driving the train, but someone is, because everything outside is fast and blurry. I can't keep up with it; I can't see to see outside the carriage window.

But in my dream, I am writing down the words of the dream. I am telling myself the story of a girl on a train waiting for her destination. She is waiting for an announcement, for someone to tell her where she is heading. I call this the Writing Dream because inside my dream I am telling myself the story of my dream, and I am writing it down so I can tell someone else. Someone like you. Because there is always someone else here, someone listening, someone reading, while I am writing it all down. But there is no paper and there is no pen, and my hands are not moving; still, I know I am writing, so somewhere there must be a notebook or a typewriter. Somehow, I am writing or typing; I listen for the clickety-clack.

I've had a notebook for years: for drawing, for doodling, for writing up lines. A doodle is a daydream, and a daydream is a break from life, a pause. Breathe in and out and the shapes will come, lines crossing under and over in most peculiar ways. A doodle is a strange dance whose steps you can never fully trace. And a doodle is the beginning of a drawing, and a drawing, if you're good enough, can become a work of art. But you need the right ingredients: a character, a story, someone worth bothering about. 'Keep your beady eyes open and your mind on the job.' Then you can report on all the missing people, because in the end we all vanish into thin air.

Take the Green Lady: she is full of ghosts, everyone says so. At night the lady in the green dress runs hither and thither. She is looking for her children; she went away and left them. When she came back, they were no longer there. Imagine losing your children. Imagine losing your name. *Serves her right for being so dilatory!* Dilatory: to delay, to procrastinate, to faff about. The stone cherub outside our house went missing one day and Mum told the policeman it was *a rob to order job*, and really, he needed to stop faffing about and find the culprit. Her cherub was more than likely in the back of someone's van on the way to Lyminster.

History is full of lost and unwanted children. There is Mary Lennox in *The Secret Garden*. Mary Lennox is a disagreeable child; she is also an unhappy child, she has good reason: Mrs Medlock, the housekeeper, who came to fetch her from the ship that brought her back to England, told her she was going to a queer place.

'You might as well know this. It's a grand but it's a gloomy place, Miss.'

How many times has that been said of old houses in the middle of nowhere, on the edge of a moor, or a stretch of fields, or high on the peak of a hill, with a large garden, and a big park all around it, with trees trailing to the ground? Misselthwaite Manor was no different from the rest: it is a state of mind; it is a way of life. Misselthwaite Manor is death: an old house with an old man and a disagreeable housekeeper, neither of whom liked children; and so, the disagreeable child, left to her own devices, begins to trespass. Behind one of the several doors, down one of the many gloomy corridors of the old manor house, she finds a gallery.

The room is full of portraits of children, little girls in long satin frocks and boys with puffed lace collars and long hair and ruffs round their necks. Mary stops to look at a portrait of a girl

in a green brocade dress holding a parrot on
her finger. The parrot is green and Mary
stares at the lustre on its wings until she begins
to feel she is turning green too. She thinks to
herself, I'm no longer sallow-skinned, I'm
green as this parrot's wings! No one can ever
call me yellow again just because I am ill. I am not
ill! I'm Mary!

A girl in a green brocade dress holding a parrot on her finger

Being pale or yellow is awful. Adults are constantly
peering at you and asking if you feel queer. 'Have you
seen a ghost?' they ask. *Plenty!* I used to say. Children
see and hear ghosts; a thin wail covered by a velvet
tapestry. Mary has heard a cry coming through the walls.
Children are always partly somewhere between ghost and
ghost, looking for stories.

And yet, sometimes a story needs an intercessory figure to
make it work: a go-between, a kindly spirit, a characterful visitor, a friend. All my life people have said, 'She's a real character',
but what does a character do? They make an appearance and
people remember them. They flounce in and out with something irresistible: charm, charisma, a steadying presence, the
voice of experience, white hair. When they are gone, they are
sorely missed. I can't say that of myself, but I can say it's true of
Mary, Mary who is settling in. I could tell you she is Mary Neal,
I could tell you she is my grandmother, or Mary Braithwaite, or
any Mary I have read about in books, because Mary is a composite character. I could tell you that Mary is my middle name,

and that all Marys meet somewhere in the middle. And I can tell you that somewhere in her life there will be ghosts keening through the walls, because history is full of lost children looking for their mothers, and children are but ghosts waiting to depart, looking for their ghostly counterparts.

The Elephant Room

MUM LIVED FOR HER GARDEN, for that view from the second floor of our granite-grey house; for the window to be open in the spring and summer; for the sea air to come wafting in. *Every room should be given a chance. Let the air in!* That was her favourite chant. Rooms were like children: you had to nurture and feed them and dress them well.

Mum's room looked over the back garden, although 'garden' is stretching it. It was a concrete runway that had been slapped out one summer; so she added window boxes and hanging baskets and suddenly the back garden was a garden centre: everything for sale. I looked from my bedroom window and saw that little purple flower, pansies with dark eyes, flowers to ease the heart; and Mum fussing and fretting and blowing on her pansies as though they were a cup of tea. Mum tried hard to ease her heart. She went without food to buy her bulbs and flowers then her marble elephants.

Once Mum had a mantelpiece full of marching marble elephants. 'Hannibal's elephants,' she said, 'the great conqueror. He crossed the Alps ever so bravely.' I looked long and hard at the elephants, but they did not move and there was no crossing. They were cold and white, frozen little beasts on the black mantelpiece. Wretchedly still. Heavy as lead, dull as ice. But they moved for Hannibal, the great conqueror, who slayed many men.

'A very brave man,' said Mum, then looked out the window towards the garden. Perhaps riding elephants through snowy mountains is brave, but I don't know why Mum wanted Hannibal on her mantelpiece, a muscly man with bare knees riding with a shield strapped to his arm. His knees looked raw and bony, chapped by the wind.

I didn't want to think of those. Instead, I thought of Mary Lennox in Misselthwaite Manor, wandering the corridors looking for treasure. Inside a lady's sitting room, Mary found a hoard of elephants. I say a room, but I mean a cabinet: a cabinet full of elephants, ivory white, all different sizes; some with mahouts and palanquins on their backs, comfy sofas for reclining in, for the ladies and gentlemen the elephants carried away, away from the cholera and malaria to the hill stations where crisp tea grew in cooler climes. My mother, a lady sipping tea on an elephant, fanned by a punkah-walla: the man who fans ladies as the elephant climbs the steep hills. What a curious arrangement, and what a curious room, full of velvet tapestries covered in strange scenes. Mary peered and saw mythical

She went without food to buy her bulbs and flowers and instead bought elephants.

beasts lunging at one another in a forest; angry bears ripping at lions' paws.

But to Mary the elephant room was unsettling; it was black and gold and heavy. Black marble, gold fenders, white elephants. An elephant afterlife, their tusks torn off by some dreadful beast. Where a black hound might suddenly bash through the window; a furious, tunnelling, cloud of grief. A place you might gnash and wail away the hours, grinding the ivory from your teeth.

Lacy curtains hung at the window and billowed like silent veils. Moths and insects died between the white layers. Nothing breathed. The window was always open, but there was no air in the room. My mother wasn't breathing, no one was breathing, not since my brother died some years ago. After that, the elephants took over and brought their funeral procession, marching left to right across the mantelpiece. But where was the thud? Elephants are large and heavy. These elephants were soundless. I stood and stared, and my heart beat loudly, because something had to. Everything was dead.

I was raised to believe in revelation. Angels and ghosts appearing behind bushes and beneath banisters. Figures underneath words once you scraped them away. Shapes left behind, spirits of place, before people began making their crude arrangements upon the earth.

But you cannot teach others to see what remains invisible; they must believe it is there: sublimity coming through the stormy clouds and air, the voice of the artist, his hand, his stare.

And now it is your stare that fills the empty space with hope and faith; turns the white void into a nativity. *What do you see? What is there?*

Hannibal the brave pushed his way through the storm. But if you look hard at the painting by the famous painter, Mr Turner, you will find Hannibal isn't there, he's missing, only his men remain. And then this huge tear in the sky. As though someone has ripped open the back of it and let all of hell through the tumult: a big white basin, a snow discus, hurling its way through an angry sky.

Underneath, the men cower; they are afraid. Soldiers should not be afraid, but the sky is one big eye looking down upon us, glaring. *Oculus*, said Miss Braithwaite who taught me how to hear and see – who gave me eloquence, some words to go looking with – but I did not expect the sky to be so big, and the sky is very big.

And in the sky in Mr Turner's painting, there is a small yellow disc, because there is always a sun when you start to tell a story. But the sun is vanishing, and the light is fading, a dark wave is curling in. Soon the men will be crushed beneath the weight of darkness, and dark is the colour of fear and dread. We must not leave them there.

'Then I said unto you, dread not, neither be afraid of them.' Do not fear what you cannot see. There is always the light of the sun overhead, the glitter of the moon and stars, the shape of the trees.

Miss Braithwaite and
the Vikings

TREES MARK PLACES. Without them you wouldn't know where you are – left or right at this lane or the next; I know a house by the shape of the tree outside. At school they taught us that a house comes with a tree. Without that old horse chestnut at the bottom of the twitten, I wouldn't remember half the places or people I knew. And I wouldn't have half the words I have because so much reading went on underneath dark boughs and branches.

Trees mark people, and branches and leaves are made from shapes and patterns – spirals and whorls and lines that split open; and we are built around such shapes and patterns which sometimes diverge at angles but nonetheless follow a Y shape, a stem that forks. They call it a fractal, but I did not know that word then, when I was still learning how to read the world; but now I say 'yes', I see, I see, I see the fork in the tree. I see the Y in the branches and leaves. So we sat beneath leafy trees and mimicked their patterns even in the way we spoke, and they marked us with their history, their branches, which words are marked with too – those forks burrowing underground along roots that diverge from person to person as they carry their words from place to place, back to the beginning – because history must start somewhere – and so it does – with a teacher underneath the trees.

At school when it was hot, they sent us outside. Miss Braithwaite said to choose your tree carefully, but there weren't many to choose from, so I dived beneath the first trunk I saw, and she was sharp and wide. Children don't notice trees at first, but trees notice them. The bark falls readily when they pluck at her. Long platelets running up and down the length of her. Brown dried-up rivers. Her flakes caught on our school cardigans. Poor Tree with her dried-up skin. No one to water her or give her food and moisture.

It was such a hot summer and Miss Braithwaite had her cardigan off, so we could see her arms; they were round and plump like dough, vol-au-vents, puffy and high, reaching up towards the sky. Miss Braithwaite was teaching us about Vikings and trees.

Make a timeline, says Miss Braithwaite. Set it all out in order. What comes first is the most important thing. First, the ancient yew tree on the Downs just above Chichester: Kingley Vale yew tree, the oldest in the country, perhaps a thousand years old, maybe two. Miss Braithwaite places her handkerchief over her head. My, it's hot today. Is everyone in the shade? Molly, shuffle up, let Katy in. We must all cover up our children. Now, our timeline. Miss Braithwaite takes a big wide yawn.

'First, the old yew tree, a thousand years old, perhaps two thousand. Her gnarled roots lie deep beneath the ground. What is a yew tree used for, Linda?'

'For killing!'

'Don't be so dramatic, Linda. You mean the yew berry is poisonous.'

'There's a bird there, Miss!'

'A little sparrow. Calm down, Katy. Open your eyes, child, we're in the middle of summer.'

But this wasn't the season for listening, and it was too hot for keeping your ears open. Our lids were heavy as lead fins. We could not swim towards Miss Braithwaite, nor away. It was too hot to pay attention, and Miss Braithwaite has a soothing voice once she gets into her stride. She calls it history, all this story-telling. How the Viking warrior Hastein came over from France to raid Sussex and roused poor King Alfred and his son, Edward, to a fight. In Appledore, in Devonshire, and then north of there, in Exeter, moving along the coast with those long boats. Gobbling things up. Raids, they call them. Viking raids. And then *besieging*, a Viking siege upon this town and the next, as they work their way along the coast. Appledore to Exeter to Wessex and Mercia and Wales. Draw the line along the hump, Miss Braithwaite says, the hip bone, East Anglia. But that was yesterday's lesson. Today we are sitting under a yew tree in the midday sun with our eyes closed and the Vikings are sailing away.

Miss Braithwaite's mouth is still moving, her head is drooping, her handkerchief has fallen onto her lap. It does not stir; there is no wind, nothing to carry us along. Viking longboats relied on the winds to push them along the coast from Devon to Wiltshire to Hampshire, then into Sussex. On the front of the boat a fierce creature was carved to frighten off the spirits of the place; a dragon or a snake to ward off their enemies. Fierce-fanged creatures sticking out their tongues at the people of Devon in their sleepy villages. People just rising from their beds. They weren't ready for such able seamen, such fierce warriors. Raiding pirates, from *vik*, meaning 'small creek or inlet', and *vikingr*, meaning 'raider' or 'pirate'. The stealthy men who came in carved narrowboats to steal gold and silver coins from churches; wool from sheep and tin from mines, although that was Cornwall. By then they were in Cornwall, the toe along the bottom. Tin comes from Cornish mines. Press the toe.

Miss Braithwaite's head was still nodding. Perhaps she knew all this off by heart – that the Vikings came along in 894 and raided Chichester. But their longboats got stuck on sandbanks in the estuary and overturned, and the people of Sussex were able to stab them in the back. Climbed over them as though they were beached whales, like that game we play at the end of the day to keep us all quiet. Dead fishes. It's hard to know who's speaking now that Miss Braithwaite has her eyes closed. And we are already dead, lying back on the stubby grass, with the leaves hanging over our faces. Dead fishes.

At the top of the tree I see a man with an axe. He's come to chop down the tree. The tree is too tall. At the top it is willowy, floating in the wind like loose ferns. Feathers. Now another man comes behind him. He hasn't an axe but a spear; the spear is long, long enough to go through one man, maybe two. How many men are there at the top of the tree? Men are piling up, I can see their bare legs, I can hear the swish of their tunics. Miss Braithwaite says that the Vikings had tidy hair and beards and clean nails, which is more than can be said for some of us here, and then her eyes roam. She never looks at me. It's funny, I can hear Miss Braithwaite in my dream.

Now she is floating up towards the sky; her hair fits the shape of the clouds, light and puffy. Vikings had good hair: short at the back and a long fringe at the front that fell over the face. Then a helmet stuck on top. Horns sticking out. A lot to wear. Heavy, must have been terribly heavy. I feel sleepy.

Miss Braithwaite is wearing a Viking helmet. I can't see her bun anymore. With her helmet on, Miss Braithwaite looks like a Viking queen. Her helmet is stuck in the trees. Those horns, they hold her; Miss Braithwaite is flying from her helmet.

'Somewhere in Sussex there is an ancient yew tree a thousand years old at least,' says Miss Braithwaite sleepily from underneath her tree. 'Perhaps two thousand years old.' How do we imagine time that old? By looking at a very old tree. You can count history by the rings of trees, how wide they are, their girth. *Girth* is a lovely word. Like *Dearth*, *death*, how many deaths has this old tree seen, I wonder? Miss Braithwaite is talking to herself. I look at the clouds.

The fighting men have gone; their raid is over. *What did they take?* Ornaments from churches. Crosses, cups, silver rings. Dropped bits of metal behind as they ran from the scene of their crime. Brass, copper, lead from the roof, coins, the collection purse. Miss Braithwaite is getting quite hot under the collar now. She's woken up. She hears something. Those thieving Vikings pummelling on church doors. A wooden knocker sounds. Someone is breaking in.

Windows

Miss Braithwaite knows all the church people because she organises church; and church is a place for showing off your best things: your best hat and scarf, your best pair of shoes, your best talking voice, the best silvery silver things for the ladies' luncheon – that lovely pair of silver salt and pepper shakers. When Miss Cull and the other ladies come in, Miss Braithwaite passes around the egg and cress sandwiches and then asks, 'Would anyone like salt and pepper?' They all say 'Yes' and Mary is pleased. Sometimes they say yes in unison like they're singing hymns.

'We're doing the Vikings this week. The names are terribly difficult to spell, let's see.'

Then Miss Braithwaite begins to recite.

'I wonder, do they worship God and say their prayers?'

'Well, they weren't *Christian*, of course, Greta.'

Miss Braithwaite likes to tell the vicar's wife that. It's always good to tell the vicar's wife that someone isn't Christian so they can make a note of it. Miss Braithwaite passes the small silver turrets around again.

'Just like little silver castles, don't you think, Dorothy? Lovely engraving work.'

She means Mrs Fortescue, Dorothy Fortescue, the lady who lives in the large house on the corner of Lobs Wood and Maltravers Drive; the one with the lions at the front gate.

'Very ostentatious,' says Miss Braithwaite when Dorothy's out of earshot. 'Lions are for the African savannah not for the corners of houses!' But the lions outside Mrs Fortescue's house are there to watch us. Suspicious beasts, they lurk, waiting for someone to pass; then lift their paws and growl. Their eyes follow me as I go by on the way to the library. Mrs Fortescue is sitting in the window looking out upon her garden. Sometimes she waves, but I try not to encourage it because I don't want her to think I'm inspecting her.

Mrs Fortescue is lonely; it must be lonely living in a large house with just a husband. Mrs Fortescue should take to writing; if you live in a large house and have time on your hands you should try to be a writer. That's what I'd do. Many stories begin with a lonely house on a moor, or in a forgotten seaside town. A place with darkened windows or curtains drawn.

You can learn a lot about people from their windows. I learned about mullion windows from Agatha Christie. *Mullion* means money and the people who want it, or the people who have it. Everyone does.

Then they pay for fancy doors and windows with brass knockers and stone arches; they put lions and eagles everywhere. Very *fortuitous*, they say,

Lions are for the African savannah not for the corners of houses!

meaning good fortune will come our way, but money usually leads to murder, the casting of aspersions: Mrs Fortescue sitting in her lonely house surrounded by a lonely garden with nothing but mullion windows to clean, waiting for something to happen. *Life can't be so empty of meaning? What do you do all day?* they say. Once, when I was ill, I feared I would lose the power of speech, all my words saved up like silver pennies. It is a terrible fear, to be wiped clean like a slate. To have nothing to say. All my pennies running away.

Write it down, Mrs Fortescue, write it down, then something will happen. Your weeds will grow at least, your forsythia bush; soon she will need clipping. In English villages, there is always an old lady clipping back a bush waiting for something to come out of hiding – *such old blooms, did you see, very established?* No, I was only passing, I didn't look, only at the lions. I always look at the lions. I thought that if I pressed down on that stone nose, that mane, I could make them talk, because writers want their characters to speak. But I shall remain silent on the subject, and Dorothy Fortescue – well, it's up to her who she tells, I wouldn't tell a soul.

But Mrs Fortescue isn't listening. Her head is turned from the window. I cannot see her face, only blank space, white pages. Somewhere inside, Mrs Fortescue's wrist is moving; her blood is flowing; she has a pulse. Her heart beats. She is writing a letter to her sister who lives far from here. Her name is Gladys, and she holds a small sword for her. Gladys, like the flower: a royal warrior, a fighter, gladiolus. Gladys will come and take her out of hiding.

It's human nature to conceal – the truth hurts – but we all

want some: bitter, salty, sweet. We gorge until our lips sting and our eyes pop open. We want our mystery; we want our novel. I have taken out three this week. *And you may well ask, what is happening? What on earth is going on here?* You are the writer after all: and now someone is knocking at the door. You must tell the policeman what it was that happened. *Do you remember, can you find your notes? Make sure you get your story straight. Can you point me towards the church?*

English churches have mullion windows and so do houses that wish to be churches; and in novels everyone is aspiring to be someone else, because once you've met a village lot of people you've met them all. Agatha Christie knew this; it's a fact that people come in sets like packs of cards. Miss Braithwaite says it all comes down to history, but *why* they did it is another matter. Motivation can be hard to determine, and circumstances play a part: those circling resentments, those hardened hearts. *Who is that passing your window?*

In Agatha Christie mysterious things often happen around doors and windows, hedges or some overgrown shrub, the climbing roses. Gardens are for covering things up: bodies, weeds, history. And garden paths are for rushing up and down – red-faced and sweaty, breathing heavily – the vicar's wife, Greta, the maid called Elsie, or Edith, May or Gladys – one of those girls. And doors and windows are for letting things out – murderers and victims, runaways and orphans – remember Jane Eyre.

Openings and closings, look out for those. *Open your bag and let it all out; the policeman wants to see everything!* But the policeman cannot see everything; I shall not share my life, the contents of my drawer. No, I will not open my bag. *Always, always, keep something back.* If you want to confess, go to church. Speak to the saints, they have many lives to shed. Mrs Fortescue nods her head.

A plot is a through-line, but life rarely follows straight through; always there is interruption, something crooked, the knock at the door: letters and telegrams, the deadly note, the body lying out. Major Fortescue understood that while you might try to march straight there are always these damn weeds in the way. I watch the major practising his parade as I pass through Lobs Wood; the major, borrowed partly from life, partly from all those mysteries I read: the concatenation of character. We stitch it all together until we have some sort of plot, some sort of life to lead. Always there is a major or a retired colonel, always there is a wife. There was in our town, swishing at the goose-grass. 'Cleavers,' Maze says; grass that cleaves to you, holds tight and won't let go. The major bashes the grass with his stick – he is not the soft and fruity sort – although in India they say he was in love with a local girl, but she ran off back to her family once the cholera broke out. Then the major lay on his bed and stared at the ceiling as the fan spun slowly. I watch the blades turning; you only need an outline or two to start a story: those spinning blades, the crisp lines of the sheets tucked into the bed. Two sets of lines, one up, one down; the ceiling and the floor, the sea and the sky, the sky and the green ground, I draw them all – those lines – and my eyes move up and down covering the person. The major is shorter than I thought, but his body is still and crumpled and I cannot see to the bottom of his legs. I am distracted by the noise. All around him there are shouts and cries, a terrible panic. People are dying, the lights in the window have gone out. It is easy to start a story, you only need a rumour, and the major carries several; and so there he lay, his face the colour of monsoon rain; they say he had fought heroically. But the ayah had run away; and then the daughter? They called her Mary because Mrs Fortescue said it was a queenly name.

Patience on a Monument

MISS BRAITHWAITE has been on holiday to see the tomb of Queen Eleanor. That's what teachers do when they go on holiday; they poke around tombs and sepulchres, all sorts of dead things. Eleanor of Aquitaine lies in the Abbey of Fontevraud with her husband, Henry II. Her second, I should say, and she bore him eight children in all, though you can never quite tell how much is rumour and how much fact. For Eleanor was tall, Eleanor was small, Eleanor was elegant, Eleanor was curvaceous, Eleanor was buxom, Eleanor was arrogant, Eleanor was lean. Eleanor was clever, Eleanor was witty, Eleanor sat upon a fine horse and rode out to crusade alongside her husband – the first one – called Louis. But Eleanor was cruel, and she got rid of Louis. What would she be wanting with him after all? Quiet, monkish, no fun at all. And then there was the problem of no son. No heir, only two daughters by Louis both fair: lovely Alix, Countess of Blois, and Marie, Countess of Champagne. Difficult women, very difficult.

They always blame the woman, says Miss Braithwaite to Edith Cull. Who's to say *the son problem* wasn't the man's problem? Eleanor was vivacious, Eleanor was bold, Eleanor was saucy, and quick to jump to Henry. Poor Eleanor was betrothed to Louis VII after her father died. Eleanor was rich, Eleanor was powerful, inheritor of all Aquitaine, Poitiers, Gascogne and others. Eleanor was capricious, Eleanor was untrue, but it was Louis who could not produce the heir. After fifteen unhappy years with the French king, Eleanor jumped ship and ran away from Paris to Poitiers to marry her cousin Henry. Eleanor was beautiful, Eleanor was brave and Eleanor was but thirty.

'Plenty of time, then,' said Miss Cull distractedly, 'to get down to business.' Miss Braithwaite narrowed her eyes. Miss Cull said the oddest things sometimes. 'I'll take a turn around the abbey, Mary, before it gets dark.'

At dusk the abbey was full of shadows. Edith liked to let them fall over her face, like tangled lace, she thought; and she kneeled and remembered Queen Eleanor. For it was the queen she thought of before she thought of God; Queen Eleanor in her mantilla veil as she prayed to God to free her from wicked men.

Eleanor in the tower weaving her web of schemes that began with hating Henry.

'But he is King of England, and he shall grant you a son!'

'Oh, Henry, how I hate you, to my very soul!'

'But you haven't married him long!'

'Oh, I never loved Louis and I never loved Henry,' she said proudly to her daughter Alice. 'No, I never loved either of them, not at all!'

There are monuments all over to dead children, and there are monuments to Shakespeare. Viola 'is every girl's favourite part,' says Mrs Rutherford quite firmly. Mrs Rutherford, who taught me how to speak Viola, says *that* heroine is a walking monument: to loss, to love, to everything she cannot have: life as a boy, life as a man, life with her love. Mrs Rutherford is *very* taken with Viola.

'Build me a willow cabin at your gate and call upon my soul within the house.' That's Mrs Fortescue speaking to her lions: poor lady, she would better love a dream.

It's better to be practical in life than to sit around waiting for the right one. Dorothy Fortescue certainly thought so. She married Henry Fortescue because he was just there, and because he seemed terribly brave and already to have life sorted. Henry's life was arranged, so why not join it? So he was sent to India and Dorothy went too, and she was only twenty. They stayed for some time. After a while she got used to the awful place. It *was* awful really, and all she could do was host parties: tea parties, bridge parties, drinks parties where everyone spoke of malaria. Then, little Mary – the child – who did better in the heat than any of them, decided it might be sensible to start school back home. Dorothy agreed. Henry agreed. So little Mary was sent to Rosemead in the centre of town, next to the convent, on the corner of the Green Lady Lane.

Nobody really knows what happened. She survived India after all, but not England. Not this sleepy little town, not that funny little school. They found her hanging from a tree. A child's body flapping in the breeze. No, *not exactly*, Miss Montgomery told the policeman, *not flapping exactly*. She'd caught herself on her petticoat. *I have no idea how it happened, officer. There are no witnesses, only other children, but you can't drag children into this.*

The horror, thought Miss Murdoch, watching from the other side of the room, *the horror of it*. Miss Montgomery was quite pale, white as a sheet. *Asphyxiation*, the policeman said slowly, I expect it's a case of asphyxiation. Could you spell the word? Miss Montgomery's spelling was usually excellent, but today the word crawled over the room and away from her like a giant spider. A-SPHIX-EE-A-TION. She would have stopped breathing after just a few moments. No pain. The policeman looked down at the floor. What a sad story to tell his wife later. She liked to hear all his stories but this one was sadder than most.

'But how on earth did it happen, Roy?' He would have to invent most of it. A child in a tree with a long petticoat. She'd got herself up onto that old flint wall. You know the one I mean, that runs along the edge of Franciscan Way: that old flint wall filled with stones.

The child must have got up to clamber into the tree. Perhaps she was after an apple. *Was it an apple tree?* The policeman scratched his head. He had no idea. They'd better find out. 'Apples,' he said slowly. 'The child was after apples.' Was she? Was she really? His wife shook her head. 'Apples aren't in season. It's too early. August, September is for apples; autumn, Roy, not spring.'

'Mmm.' The policeman scratched his head. The lady with the fine grey hair (he could be very observant when he wanted to be) looked worried, very worried. (He wrote that down.) She would be.

'I'd be if I were 'er,' he said to his wife Martha. 'I'd not get a moment's rest, not a minute of shut eye with that child's pale face and bobbing head on me mind.'

'Oh Roy, shhh. Don't be frightening me.'

'That poor lady. I do feel terribly sorry for 'er.'

'The parents.'

'The parents.'

And they sat and sipped their tea loudly to cover up the thought of the child in the tree.

'If that 'appened to our Tommy.'

'Shh, Mart. Don't be 'avin' such thoughts.'

'That poor lady will be though.'

'Mrs Fortescue?'

'Even grand people have feelings.'

When children die people build monuments. If you're grand, you can bag a place in the church, so Mrs Fortescue insisted that Mary's monument be made from brass. Like Patience, she sat on her monument, smiling at grief. *Patience* is a quiet sort of word, but grief is never so. It screams. Mrs Fortescue hit the brass bell next to her with her glove. She must hit something. Was this the bell for mass? She thought that was Catholic, but perhaps Protestants did too. In any case, it was a sweet little bell; she would hit it again. And again. And Dorothy Fortescue sat and hit the bell, over and over, for quite some time. She took off her glove and hit it with her fist. A most peculiar thing to do. Over and over, until her knuckles hurt and that interfering woman, the vicar's wife, who always wanted something from her, came running down the aisle.

Mrs Robinson

SOME PEOPLE never make it into life: they remain stuck and frozen behind glass. Waxworks. Butterflies pinned to velvet cushions. Stuffed birds, their heads cut off. Somewhere between life and death, they hover, where there is no living thing. Preserved behind glass for someone else's fancy. Someone else's life.

Mrs Robinson is hard to see behind the smeary glass. She comes and goes like a shadow upon the lawn, but I can never see her face. She sits in the back drawer of Boots the Chemist like an undeveloped negative. 'Nothing to see there, dear, nothing but blanks, I'm afraid she didn't come out.' Mrs Robinson never comes out; she has no shape, no outline, so where do you start?

VIOLA: A blank, my Lord, she never told her love.

I wonder who Mrs Robinson loves, what makes her heart sing?

Some people leave no traces, no papers, no archive. Mrs Robinson left only her thin shadow on the smeary glass, but her shadow has photographed better than anything I have ever seen or heard. Mrs Robinson shines brightly through my windowpane.

Jack Robinson never bought his wife flowers, not her whole entire bleeding life. So Joan Robinson who looked down from the floor above us wondered what the woman below was doing with all those baskets hanging from the wall. Joan in her eggy nightie, because what was the point of washing something more than once a fortnight if you were going to wash it again? And Joanie, as her mother called her, or Moanie as he often did, pushed up the window with her wooden spoon and began her long think about her pretty neighbour watering her flowers.

Those petunias will need a lot of drink now the sun's decided to pay us a visit. Lobelia and wild geraniums flapping around like flags. *It's like the Jubilee down there.* And Mrs Robinson, once called Joanie, twists her body towards the window and frowns down upon the fair-haired woman going about her business: lifting her can and letting the water fall in a nice sprinkle over those wire baskets clipped to the wall. Quite tight, quite high, it's a wonder she can manage. Now who's that? *Go on, help your Ma, there's a good girl! Oh, I've got a crick in me neck! Let's have some coffee.* Joan Robinson pulls back the net curtain.

Coffee Time. Enough peeking. How much milk do we have? Enough milk for a whole cup at least. He'd bring more tonight, that at least. She never had to ask, so there wasn't even that to discuss. Not even eggs, milk and a loaf of bread after all these years. *Now where's me coffee jar – in the same place, Joanie, always in the same place, on the shelf behind the sink.* One, two, three small spoonfuls of desiccated coffee, Joanie likes it strong – and look, there's the Queen.

The Queen on me coffee cup.

What on earth does that mean?

And Joanie leans against the sink and looks out through the grey veil. *Bleedin' winders need a clean.*

A faint hissing from behind. *The milk! Caught you just in time! In you go!* A shout from outside the window: a child's voice from the back of the house. She'd go and look. No harm in looking. And Joan Robinson shuffles down the three stairs that separate the kitchen from the hallway. Already the milk was cooling in the dark, already her fingers stiffening. She closed her eyes and held her breath. Corridors frightened her, long dark tubes you stared down; she could never feel the end. When was the end coming? *Mama, Mama, where is the end?*

Childish, childish, childish, Joanie! Moanie, moanie, moanie Joanie! Where are yer going with that man?

Another cry from outside; a faint square letting in a fraction of light. More cries, and sun breaking through the polyester. She'd take a peek. *Won't stay long, just have a quick look.* Now lift your legs up, Joanie, come on, *quick march, stride forth!* She used to, Joanie used to: march across the fields from school, through the wheat and barley and the poppies in July. Past the delicate poppies that lost their wings so easily: with the brush of her skirt, with the touch of her finger, with one small blow from her mouth. With, with, with. *Who was Joanie Robinson with?*

A large lumbering man. Can you see her, passing through the fields? She is with some man. A tall dark column of a man, passing through the fields with her. Soon she will be with child.

Who said that? To be with child so young is sinful. Don't say that! Joanie Robinson, where are you going? Who do you belong to now? That little slip of a thing in her thin chequered school dress ripped at the hem: from climbing fences, from clambering trees, *Joanie Robinson, the state you're in!*

You can't keep clean in the country. *You can't, you can't.* Stop nagging all those country children. They have their own ways of mucking in. Buttercups and daisies and dandelions; stickle weed stuck to cowpats. Berries squashed between their hands, mouthfuls.

What else were children for but sunshine and daisy flowers? Joanie pulls at the hallway curtains; the fair-haired children were below, three of them playing catch with a yellow ball. How much she'd like to be sitting down there in the sun picking daisy flowers. She'd make them chains. Do they know how to make daisy chains? Delicate, delicate things, and Joan Robinson shut her eyes and began to dream of daisy flowers.

She sometimes had these daydreams. *Day's eyes*, they call them when the day suddenly bores dark holes. They came to her abruptly; in dark rooms, when the curtains were drawn, when dusk was drawing in, when she lay under the covers at night listening to him snore. Then she saw white flowers filled with yellow smiles sitting upon green lawns. A pair of small pink hands, cupped, a blue sky behind and above – daisy flowers talking to her, telling her their secrets: who fancied who, and who had come a-courting.

Daisies weren't half as common as you thought. Born into the star family, they send their seeds abroad, to all sorts. So she took him and kissed him under covering of his black hair and she thought then, how much he looked like a raven. But her sisters said *yes, yes, yes, yes, you must must take him*, the younger siblings and the old, they all said *yes*, though they had not heard of that other history of the daisy flower: *woundwort, bruisewort, trampled-upon*, after those bruising boys spat all over her yellow face. She went to school with them, and they were tough and spiky and ripped at her stigma and pulled at her petals, made her white collar filthy by their beefy hands.

He loves me, he loves me not, he cares for me, he cares not. She believed him, and a man must have a wife, a farmer must have a farmer's wife, and so she said – *I care for you, he loves me true.*

Joanie, they called her, though really she should have been *Marguerite*, sat alone at home withering, and her pistil withered too, all those female parts. And her pappus bristled, but nothing came, no pollen, no seed; and so he never touched her again but turned his hands to implements with sharp blades.

Something stirred on the neighbour's wall: a sparrow, Joanie heard the tweeting. Her daydream did not include many birds. She was too fond of birds to make them part of her dream. Birds came to the windowsill, and she fed them with crumbs kept inside a cellophane bag. She hid it in the kitchen drawer. *All her silly turns*, he called them. *Saving the birds*, she called it. *Protecting the little ones.* RSPB. An envelope had come through once. She found it under the kitchen table and scooped it up. Put it in her apron pocket, that old raggedy thing she wore over her nightie.

Once he'd ask her to take it off and she did, just like that, in the middle of the kitchen floor. A scraggy old bird standing there shivering, her bones chattering through her feet. After a while we are only birds and mice, waiting for the cat to pounce.

Mrs Robinson is growing cold, Mrs Robinson is growing old. Where are you now, Joanie Robinson? Still at your window?

Have you been eaten by the cat? Our cat. Sleek, with a black and white butler's bib; you watched him stalk through the grass like a tiger.

I wonder what they're feeding him on. Cats like tuna but I doubt he's getting that down there, thought Mrs Robinson as she stared down at us from the third floor. You were always looking.

And we were always *down there*, and you were always *up there*. *The Robinsons*. But I think you always liked us, Mrs Robinson, and given half the chance you'd have come skipping down the stairs to play with us, to stroke the cat and sing us songs, to take us to the beach. And we would no longer have been *them down there*. *So many children and no fathers. So many people dressed in odd-coloured clothes.* You would have heard it all, the wailing coming through the walls. Religion does funny things to people, and you must have wondered, Mrs Robinson, of course you did, what on earth we were all doing down there with God sitting on the front-room floor. Legs crossed, gas fire on, curtains closed. Always a sign, the curtains, always closed. And the woman with the dark hair, and the woman with the blonde, and the old woman dragging in her bicycle. She had a sweet smile.

Mind your own business, he said, but Joanie Robinson could hear the murmuring coming through the floors. Voices vibrating,

ribbit ribbit ribbiting frogs

[74]

ribbiting like frogs; a pond full of frogs on the floor. Louder and louder until they began to sing and wail as the sun went down. Hot crayons melting – waxy frogs – why did she keep thinking of frogs? They boiled them in France. Hotter and hotter, she thought, they must be terribly hot. Coloured pencils melting. Then when one day they disappeared, all snapped in two.

Jack Robinson

WHO WILL LET Mr Robinson out? He is stuck inside a frame on the outside of our house, that's where I see him. On the front steps climbing down, hand hovering over the bell. Mr Robinson, will someone let you in? Answer the bell! Mr Robinson, you had a childhood too; why have we forgotten?

I blame the spade. Mr Robinson bore a spade over his shoulder wherever he went; like a petty criminal, like a murderer, we thought him a filthy sort. His accessory outdid him: it was too much, too large for him to bear. But I must give Mr Robinson a second chance. Turn him around, follow him to the back of the house, back to the beginning. Mr Robinson, you came through the front door, but I know you grew in our twitten, like the dry soil. Jack Robinson, you are one of our folk, and we are a filthy lot.

Bath day was Sunday but there was only enough water for one. Eight dirty ducks splashing around in a tin bath, the water was cold before you could say Jack Robinson. To this day Jack's reluctant to use water, wears one pair of overalls throughout the week. She hangs them up to drip dry in the bathroom and they take all night. Is that a body in there dripping away, bleeding? Mrs Robinson has a grim imagination, or perhaps it's Mr

Robinson, they are in it together. One body begets another, but the tin bath turned everyone into a bird splashing about in cold water. Dirty birds left out in the filthy rain, flapping.

And meanwhile, all night long the trousers drip and hang, drip and hang, until Mr Robinson barges in in the morning – so his wife says, doing her teeth – to do his First Thing in the Morning Business – to find the trousers no longer hanging limp but stiff as a piece of old cardboard. Stiff as a rusty old drainpipe, stiff as an early morning body waking up from the dead.

'Let them soak in the sink then,' says Mrs Robinson, *grrrr, that man*, and she bites her toothbrush until her jaw begins to ache. That's what bitterness does to you, and Mrs Robinson is bitter, for she's been locked up with this old git for years, and for years before that if you count those lived next door.

History is full of unwanted children. Joanie O'Grady remembers the Robinsons and their old tin bath because she used to look over the garden wall and watch them *at their ab-loo-shuns*, her father said. *Dirty little buggers*, said Mr O'Grady, that's what he said, her father. Irish name, came via Liverpool, came over on mucky old liners, always mucky wherever they went. Then some of those filthy feathered creatures flew down to Sussex and found themselves grubbing for worms down a twitten with buttercups and celandine clinging to the walls. Worm-eaters, that's what we called them, said Joanie, before it was too late to say Jack Robinson, before it was too late to say Mrs Robinson who lived on the top floor, looking down over the twitten like a silent statue.

The twitten that was here long before we were and grew all sorts of things. *It's the bulbous buttercup that grows along the twitten*, Maze says. And now, I have learned her words, my grandmother's words. *A perennating perennial herb that will keep on year after year*, season after season, growing, spreading, laying to waste other herbs and weeds. The bulbous buttercup is planning her next siege, from April to June, when she opens her golden cups to the sun, and flowers. She has been around a long time: far longer than the Jack Robinsons of this world who began life banging about in a draughty outhouse with sawdust sticking to their *nether regions* (anything dark and dank; an underworld). Filthy hands and faces smelling of carbolic soap, and never a clear nail on their finger, not one – all lined with black soil, dark little ridges in the foothills of white, speckled with milky dots from lack of this and that – *zinc*, Maze said, those spotted white dots, two eyes peering up at him. They show on our nails, because we are perennials too.

And I want you to imagine that before Mr Robinson there was Jack Robinson, the boy shivering in two inches of bath water. Always the last to go. The last to have his bath in that damp and draughty shack of a place behind the house on Wick Farm Road where crab apples fell on the roof and branches broke a hole right through. So they stuffed it with twigs and leaves until Mr Jarvis heard them, the gentleman who walks with a funny stick and bangs on the fence when they're out larking about after school. Or sometimes when one of them is on the privy he bangs with his stick against the metal wall, and so they bang back, those boys. They bang and bang with the wooden stick left by the privy to stir in sawdust and ashes, sometimes leaves, though Mam says it's better to stir in bits of bark to try to keep things dry. But boys never listen, not at that age, so they tip out the bucket upon the ground and the putrid liquid runs everywhere. All over the daisy flowers, their heads flung back and screaming, their crowns ripped off, their petals clinging together and chanting, *he loves me, he loves me not, he loves me, he loves me not. A composite flower,* says Miss Braithwaite, *her petals stick together, she is made of several parts.* As selves are, and histories, until it is time to fold ourselves away and sleep.

A Brief Biography

AFTER SLEEP there is the day, and the day is a miniature biography, and a biography is a story of someone's life told by someone who knows you. Take Mary. On Sundays she goes walking, an event too small to recount, you say. Why bother to count those minute moments walking to and fro: the gathering of her knapsack, the tying of her shoes, the brief and dull biography of an unclasped day? But Mary knows where she's going, and she knows just what she's doing; she always has, she always will, in this world and forever.

She knows so much of life begins and ends sitting in a chair. Mary's day starts on a stiff-backed chair tying her shoes, and then on a lurching train. The seat is hard, she remembers that; nothing is yielding. Nonetheless she is *on* her seat: she is on a seat on the train putting herself together. *On*, that is the point. Mary is moving on towards her day which is passing. Onwards and onwards until days later, years later, we begin to wonder what about today makes this a day? But by then, it's too late: the day's eye has disappeared, the daisy flower closed and gone to sleep, long gone underground, on and on and on.

Meanwhile, Mary is gathering herself into her day; she is building her centre, drawing herself into that yellow disc, as the sun shines down through the carriage window, and she turns to look at the yellow fields out through the window. Out and out and out towards the yellow. Corn, wheat, barley, she wonders. When the sun dances circles across her lap she knows the day has started. *She is on her way, my character. I have found her; I have adopted her. Perhaps now she will adopt me. Sunny Mary, I call her, a pink daisy flower. An evergreen.*

It is a complicated journey to Amberley where the old castle sits above boggy fields. Soon Mary will pass through those fields and listen to the squelch of her shoes as the mud sucks them in with her mouth. Yes, the mud has a mouth; as we do. Mary's shoes are robust, they are waterproof, and she has worn them for years. They are the shoes her mother wore, and she will pass the castle in her mother's shoes, and they will open their mouth and speak of things they saw on that day in Amberley. The castle: a craggy edifice with high walls. High walls to keep out their enemies; the bishops of Chichester used it as a fortress to keep away their enemies: this is what she tells them, the children. Children like the sound of enemies and so they draw Amberley Castle because they enjoy its boxy, cakey shape, its high walls.

Poor Amberley: soon it will be a hotel laid with plush carpets. Dark so as not to show the stains: coffee, red wine, a rare Bordeaux; several glasses of orange juice, and a dry Martini that went tumbling down the stairs! Oh, how the wealthy travel, with so much stuff! Tripping in with their suitcases and chauffeurs – or rather the porter does – carrying the cases up to their rooms as he lifts his cap, holds out his invisible hand, the invisible man who lightens their burden.

It is always best to travel light, thinks Mary as the train bounces along, as the green fields whip up and down making her giddy; and she stands for a moment to open the window because she'd like to have some of that green scent come in and over. Breathe, Mary, breathe. She looks at her feet and squeezes her toes; it is a reassuring gesture, not worth recording, but it's important to know she is here and now clasping her knapsack, feeling her bones. No one will remember it once she is dead, no one ever could: how she held tight to her canvas bag that bright morning in April with this life racing along – her pulse – and this train jerking up towards the chalky hills with Mary, head flung from the window, in search of green.

MARY NEAL: A GREEN LADY
'She brought into the atmosphere the sparkle
of a clear, frosty, winter day.'
(Description of Mary Neal by Roy Judge)

Writers must acknowledge their sources, and Mary is a composite character. She is also a historical one. Born in 1860, as Clara Sophia Neal, Mary has an archive. In the entries you might read, Mary is often described thus: social worker, educational reformer, suffragette, committed teacher of folk music and dance, a folk revivalist, an arts practitioner, a devout champion of working-class girls. Mary Neal, who set up a club for seamstresses in the slums of Somers Town. Sister Mary of the West London Mission, a woman of faith and substance, a woman of character. A strong mind, a lusty voice, she taught them how to dance and sing, her girls. She gave them *espérance* – hope – she gave them the Espérance Club. She gave them Shakespeare.

Soon after leaving the mission – the rules became too stifling – she bought a house with the help of two other women, Emmeline Pethick-Lawrence and Lily Montagu – the Green Lady Hostel situated on the Green Lady Lane in Littlehampton next to my school. These are her summary facts.

But I like to think of Mary like this: foster mother, muse, spirit of place, kindly ghost. A social worker, a woman prepared to roll up her sleeves and muck in, for muck is what she found inside those filthy homes in Soho. Sinks stacked with dirty vessels, the stench of unwashed clothes, bodies crushed together, and enough children to fill a small school. Tired and complaining from hunger and cold. So she took a few of the older girls back with her to her club which met in Cumberland Market behind St Pancras and Euston a few evenings a week. Tuesdays and Thursdays, and then some Fridays too. *It is never enough, Emmeline, it is never enough, those few hours a week of singing and dancing. Their bodies are racked with nerves.* It is never enough to turn the din of the machine into a tune. Those tunes she woke to every morning from her sleep. *And beauty born of murmuring sound shall pass into her face,* the poet says. *And vital feelings of delight. Shall rear her form to stately height.*

Mary knew that life is made of many moods and sudden shifts in time and place. The straight line through is never true. Threads can unexpectedly snap and break. The parts of you are scattered; there are strange zigzags. Only the light of the imagination can see you through, that strong torch shining through the dark.

In the photograph I've found of her she is square-jawed and handsome; a pearly light shines from her necklace. I stare at

Mary and the corners of her mouth turn up. She turns to me and smiles.

'After the war I decided I needed a rest, to live in complete rural isolation, and so I took a small-thatched cottage in Amberley with no running water, not even a drain or a tap. But before many weeks had passed I found I had a small boy of six years old living with me and one a year older, and before long they had acquired a dog, a cat, a goat, a rabbit and a parrot. I tried to find some domestic help but all the women in the village appeared to be busy letting rooms to artists who loved to come and paint the village. And so my time of rest vanished and I began another sort of life for which I did not feel at all suited. The backache! When every evening I carried up kettles.'

Artists must go in search of something to fill the dark, a radiant subject. Joseph Mallord William Turner always carried a light with him, and his light was made of primary colours, yellow, red and blue, orange and green, the colours you see when the light is split open. To these he added white and black for shape and tone, for texture and movement. Yellow and white were his stalwarts, his favourites, because they were the clouds, the sun, the light, the haze, and they allowed him to peer, to hope, to strain to see. Sea mist, fog and fire, the light coming up in the morning.

My grandmother on her bicycle in winter, head bent over, plastic sou'wester on, riding into the wind. She is a small, barely perceptible figure, and Mr Turner would have seen only the bicycle wheels spinning and the splash of water from the overnight puddles as her tyres ran through them, down Norfolk

Road and onto Selbourne and Irvine, left onto Granville Road. But roads were immaterial, all that mattered was the light, and my grandmother always had the dawn light because she was the first to stir, carrying with her pints of milk, loaves of bread to feed us. She had the birds and the first signs of weather; she had the wind and the rain clinging to her soft white hair as she hauled her bicycle up the steps of our granite house by the sea. Right on the corner, almost, Mr Turner might have noticed that, because of the angle, but he would not have paid much attention to her ascent. He may have glanced up at the tall sash windows across three floors and given a quick flick of his wrist across his ivy white paper, a small line or two, just to remember, if he could find his granite pencil. And if he had the mind to crick his neck up slightly, he would see that the curtains were all drawn. And not just because it was still dawn, but because the people of this house did not wonder how light travelled through glassy windows or across stone terraces or how it was interrupted by flying buttresses on the corners of churches or the faces of gargoyles pointing their tongues rudely down upon the people. Mr Turner would only wonder why on earth they never gave the light a chance: that shaft of milky sunshine as my grandmother opened the front door and stepped into the dark hallway – the hallway which would be too dark for him, the stairs too narrow and compressed – and Mr Turner would begin to wonder what hope there was for a place that could not hold any red and orange, any yellow and white flames stirring into fiery life. He would shrug his shoulders, sigh, and walk away across the green, towards the pebbly beach, the flint wall.

Over the Wall

THE GARDEN OVER the road had a high wall. Down below were thick green bushes good for hiding in. Yew with woody parts sticking up like razors; impossible to pass through, so we cut a hole. They hurt us, but we wanted the green. To touch it, to suck its wings. The garden of the Beach Hotel was full of people we had never seen. I wanted to climb through and touch the soil. Touch the palm trees, the yew trees. Touch *their* green.

Dry branches leaving red crosses. *Taxus baccata*, the prickly yew tree. Sharp green needles their leaves. She carries red berries in her hands – a goddess once – who got stuck between this wall and her roots snagged into sharp flint. Artemis, goddess of the hunt, snatching at the berries, dipped her arrows into their poison to kill her enemies. **Red:** the colour of poison, the colour of death, the colour of red arrows shooting into the dawn; a deer lying dead on its side; the goddess wiping her hands. I climbed over the red berries and wiped my hands on the waxy leaves. **Green:** the colour of life, the colour of grass stains on my

Yew – green needles their leaves

Taxus baccata, the prickly yew tree
Sharp green needles their leaves

[86]

white clothes as I jump to the ground; my socks rubbing against the green blades; the mulch of cuttings left behind by the gardener, the grounds man, the man with his cap on I've seen going to and fro with a lawnmower pressing the whirring blade into the ground.

The blade is turning fast, and the man is huffing and puffing across the tufty grass, all mixed up with sand blown in from the beach. He is sweating; I can see the beads running down his nose into his mouth. He is licking up his sweat. I will run across the grass when he isn't looking to the side of the hotel. I will run through the green and it will smudge between my toes. Green: the colour of dare. *Dare devil*, they said – my brothers – who I left behind. Green: the colour of trespass, the colour behind my eyes when I close them, green and prickly and *hard*. My feet touch it, my hands too; it lies on the other side of the wall. Green: the colour of children jumping into the air. I land, and the man looks up and wipes his brow. He does not see me through his beads of sweat; they are too thick and warm, eggs cooking on his nose and eyelids. I run, back to the beginning, towards the green, the first colour I saw lying on the grass.

Now if you want to get back to the beginning you must come a different way, with the child in mind. She knows the ground is there. She can feel it with her soft feet; they pad across the words – towards, because we must always go somewhere, life must have a plot – so go towards the child who pushes through the words, thick and woody and layered. Green and shiny, they fall on her face, and she cannot see her way through the sunlight, through the thick hedge, through and through with her strong hands picking at the words that fall and shed as she clambers down to fetch them down and down and through the yew leaves. Taxus baccata, *the tree of death, of Hecate, goddess of the underworld, who moves with red berries crushed in the palm of the hand, who pushes through the soil towards the child who sees all the colours of life and death.*

Red: *the colour of my grandmother's finger after she rubs her Christmas cactus plant for luck. Dabs it with cotton wool and wraps around a plaster. Red peeks out on top, paler, thinner, mixed with pink, my grandmother's skin. Red: the colour of the slap left on my cheek. Green: a child left unwrapped.*

Red and green: *the colour of words before you add anything to them: life, history, all that talk of meaning.*

Red and green: *Christmas, what does that ever mean?*

Red and green *are brassy then and the church bells ring.*

Red poinsettias *in the shops and the church porch, some fading to pink, the gentler sort.*

The colour of memory before you add seasoning, a certain way of seeing words on the page with the white foamy sea washing around them, full of intention, dying to know, always dying to know.

As you lay out *in the garden, five minutes from the sea, keen to join the shingle and salt wind, the quiet pat of the sand, the shoreline, photographed from pure joy of seeing the sun fall on the waves and the promenade lying out long and hard along the breakwaters.*

This is your garden too,
with only a flint wall and a road in the way:
pushing hard against the soil.

*

That wall held history. Jammed between its flinty stones was another story. Four years ago, or was it five, we went to the Beach Hotel with Mum and Dad. On Valentine's Day in 1980 Dad took Mum out for dinner to try and make things up, to make it all up to her, his going away. He took her out for dinner, the night Mum nearly got away from the woman upstairs. You've heard of her before, you just need to read more. Adults were always saying that, reading leads to higher things: that book, this wall, higher and higher I climb.

But she didn't leave, because Dad wasn't the sort to be making marriage proposals; and he wasn't the right sort of person to be seen at the Beach Hotel. Not then, not now, not ever. Whereas Mum was, she looked the part. Mum had the right sort of greeting: a warm firm smile, peachy and splitting open; a smile that held you to attention; the waiter and his trembling hands, the silver in the basket, the shape of the candle flickering back and forth over her face. It was winter, 14 February 1980, and we were sitting around a table at the Beach Hotel waiting. The lights were very low.

If you turned the lights up, you'd see that in 1980 the Beach Hotel was in bad repair. Somebody has dropped the reins, dropped the leash, let the staff go. And that was when they let us in, the poor dogs who lived off the alley. Woof, woof!

Just as the wallpaper was beginning to peel in the smart drawing room, as the blue and white china cups were starting to chip under their lips, and the handle to the back gate was turning wonky from being pulled too hard by cheery maids coming and going over the years. Sassy girls with sharp chins and wagging fingers dismissing their lovers out of hand: the butcher boy, the ironmonger, the lad who brought the fish – all sent packing. Too many comings and goings, too many changes of hands – the details keep slipping – the bolts, the locks, the chains, the bright metal world that keeps the wrong sort out; that keeps the hotel show on the road. Curtains up, curtains down, and in between the well-rehearsed performance – everyone knows their lines, their cues. Before the gaps began to show, the Beach Hotel was a terribly nice place to go. Everyone said so.

A genteel space, for older ladies and film stars looking for recuperation – or preparation – for their big role. Somewhere to take the sun and sea air, to order tea and cocktails and a spot of luncheon and do whatever didn't get on your nerves. Unfold the newspaper slowly, glance at the headlines, spend the morning with the crossword in the front lobby. Never mind what anyone was doing on the outside. Time drifted nonchalantly by and you didn't blink an eyelid or turn a hair.

You could grumble at the squawk of the seagulls and stuff a handkerchief in the draughty window, but nothing would be asked of you except to remember to come down for your tea. Order a car when you need one; take a stroll along the prom; meet up with old acquaintances upon the green; buy an ice and sit beneath the parasol out along the front. Watch the waves, shoo away the seagulls, skim stones along the shore (only for the young ones). Turn around and amble back towards the Victorian villa set back from the shore.

PART THREE

Inventing Lives

The Harbour Folk

IN THE OLD PHOTOGRAPHS of Littlehampton the people on the pier stand around in Victorian clothes looking awkward and uncomfortable. Nobody speaks: they are too busy watching; a large ship is coming in.

High white sails, stiff and formal, look down upon the shuffling people. Arms outstretched, they are dead birds, and she is full of ropes, rigging. The birds flop and fall forwards, their heads hang on the black nets. The rigging catches them, and the wind pushes out the sails, something falls into the river. The man wearing his cap leans over the harbour wall.

'Can yer see anything, Pete?' The woman sitting opposite him peers down into the water but the weeds cover her view. Her back is turned to the brig; she is not there to see the ship. She has come to the harbour to discuss marriage. Mabel Pegrum wants to see her ring. 'When we gonna get married, Pete? You been dragging your feet?' But the sound of her asking is drowned out by the paddle wheels turning on the steamboat that pulls the great brig. Pete watches the big ship come in. Mabel prods him but her prodding is too late for a proposal. Pete and Mabel will never marry, because a few months from now he will take a job at sea repairing rigging. Mabel reaches for his hand, but his hand is sheltering his eyes, eyes that follow the ship steering its way in, eyes that look towards the sun.

Everything in this picture is the wrong size. The lighthouse at the end of the promenade is too small for the ship, the ship is too large for the lighthouse, for the harbour, for the people. But the people have come down to the harbour to look; they have come to watch the ship pass through, to stare at the little tug boat, *Jumna*, as she boldly pulls the huge brig, the *barquentine*, or schooner barque, a ship with three large sails fore and aft.

It is a fine day in August and the people on the pier have come to watch the big ship sail through. It is 1895 and the harbourmaster is standing on the edge of the pier with his cloth cap on; he feels a sudden well of pride: the brigantine *Ebenezer* will sail into harbour today too. She will bring coal from Newcastle for the gas works on Pier Road and the brewery on the High Street. The people on the promenade sit and stand around expectantly. On the edge, towards the lighthouse, there is a middle-aged woman with a strong jaw. Next to her stands a tall and elegant woman, her companion, judging by the narrow space between them. They are visitors, while the people around them are local. Men strolling with hands behind their backs or resting against the wall; women standing erect, their hats turned sideways – this is a photograph after all – it only takes one to start to speak.

The harbourmaster turns to the gentleman in the straw hat to ask his opinion of events: the sound of the boat chugging along and the sight of the steam billowing behind, sooty and black, filling the air.

'She's got a real load there!'

'She certainly has. Such a little boat pulling such a huge brig.'

'With all those people too. How many do you count? Fifteen, I reckon.'

The gentleman in the straw hat turns to look at the man with a beard. A real sea captain, he thinks, as the man in the cloth cap removes his hat and scratches his head, while the man taken for a sea captain begins to speak.

'We haven't had such a large brig come through for a while, not for a month or two. From Newcastle, on her way to Portsmouth, carrying coal.'

The gentleman in the straw hat looks again at the man scratching his head and begins to place him.

'Drummond . . . the harbourmaster. Pleased to meet you.'

'Pleased to make your acquaintance, sir.'

The gentleman does not give his name, but Drummond doesn't notice. He's too busy looking at the ships, marking their progress. By now *Jumna* has docked into her berth and the enormous brig is moored behind her. Soon they will begin to unload her, and the people on Pier Road will peek out from behind their curtains and comment on the number of sacks they see piling up along the harbour wall. Children passing by will count them and their mothers will pull them away. *Leave them alone, Tommy, they're nothing to do with you!*

The year I was born, or the year after, a bridge appeared over the River Arun: a red retractable bridge which opened in the middle to let ships under. That was the bridge that split in two, but before the red bridge, there was another. In 1905, a swing bridge was built across the river. That was the year Mary Neal brought her girls down from Somers Town, London, to stay at the Green Lady Hostel. The year the girls crossed the bridge holding onto their hats and screaming, laughing, and tipping this way and that. Years later, the swing bridge was taken down. Too dangerous, they said, far too many accidents, so it was dismantled, and the red bridge came along.

On the other side was Rope Walk, because once, even before the swing bridge, there was a bridge made from rope; a flimsy tacked together one of slats and knotted rope.

In the summer, a ferry went back and forth, a wooden raft with oars, and men rowed across the river drinking coffee from billycans. I remember them. The men were laughing, and the sun fell on their faces. I looked down into the water to avoid their gaze, and the sunlight made my eyes squint. Men laughing and smirking, and their laughs are strange. I am not familiar with those mouths, the way they turn up towards the sun, like little suns themselves. Cheeky grins, with eyes that come and go. They shade their eyes, deep green and brown, eyes the colour of beer.

Men dragging their boat up towards the harbour wall where they tie the bow to cleats; their rope is strong and covered in weed, which follows in with the tide. Then come the crabs when no one can see them, upon the high tide. Then seagulls, cormorants and small white egrets. At low tide the crabs hide beneath the rocks, then Phyllis and Elsie and Florrie scramble down and kick at the green rocks left behind.

Florrie isn't frightened and neither is Phyllis. Crabs can't do anything to them. Phyllis is fearless, but Elsie is not. Elsie is a whimperer. She is doing it now because she has bashed her toe and the others are getting ahead of her. Florrie and Phyllis are clearing the harbour wall, while Elsie is struggling to keep up; she is clambering over the rocks that are getting bigger and bigger. *Ow-wee, ow-wee*, says the girl in her white smock, though she isn't very white anymore.

Elsie is turner greyer and greyer, green, and grey, now black. There is tar at the bottom of the river, and it drags across her, the hem of her skirt drinks it in, and now Elsie's skirt is soaked. Soaked Elsie carries on clambering over the pebble and rocks. Soon she is at the end of the swing bridge where the rocks are huge and pointed. A man stands on the other side of the bridge and stares, his head tilts up and down. You will get dizzy if you watch him. His hands are moving up and down, flying.

Elsie can't see him, but I can, and Mary can too, for she has her binoculars out. Mary is peering across the river at the man who is painting the swing bridge: it is majestic, it is glorious in the sun, and the man's hand is moving up and down. And look! There is Elsie Turner! He can make out her small white bonnet, her moving shape. Crabs aren't white, they are dark pink, turning brown, but if crabs were white, Elsie Turner would be one.

Elsie looks up and sees the men crossing in the ferry – they are waving – they are waving at Elsie. Oh, how happy she is! The men take turns to wave at the other girls on the pier, but Elsie does not notice, she is apart. Elsie would like to remain apart. All her life, Elise will say, 'I would like to remain apart and let others find me.' It is a consoling thought, and it is Elsie's thought. She will carry it for years.

Meanwhile, the girls look back at the men; they are laughing and waving, they are giggling. It is nice to be looked at by men, and the men think so too, and so they wave and laugh and laugh and wave and swig from their green bottles and pull themselves up upon the weeds. Behind the girls stand three women wearing bonnets – it's the first thing you see – white birds tumbling over their faces. The sun glances sideways, bounces left and right from around their straw-bound sides, along their skirts, running from behind like whipped cream. On top of each bonnet are feathers: the wind pulls and tugs and the feathers brush over her face because it is the tall lady I notice first, her feather, and then her wide grin. Her name is Constance, and she has come down for the summer to stay with her friend, Mary Neal.

'Now come along, girls, it isn't seemly to wave at men like that,' says Lady Constance Lytton. 'Let's go along the pier and see what the waves are doing.'

'Let's have a song,' says Mary. 'Florrie, will you begin?'

'I dunno th' wurds yet.'

'Yes you do, Florrie. We'll help you.'

Alas my love, you do me wrong,
To cast me off discourteously . . .

Mary's voice is strong.

'What does "dis-curt-tis-ly" mean,' says Elsie, who is refusing to hold Florrie's hand.

'Poor manners, lacking in grace,' says Constance, tilting her head towards the children. 'Shoulders nice and straight, Elsie.'

'Rude,' says Mary firmly. 'Unseemly and rude.'

'Like that boy we saw th'uver day gawpin' up at us! Gawpin' and gawpin' like he'd niver seen gels dancin' before. Must've got a crick in his neck from gawpin' so long.'

'Shh, Florrie, not so loud. Save your lungs for singing.'

Alas my love, you do me wrong,
To cast me off discourteously.
And I have loved you oh so long,
Delighting in your company.

And their voices trail away as they proceed towards the white pillar on the edge of the pier.

People wander. They travel from room to room, from place to place, and you cannot follow. No matter how many maps you consult, how many lines you draw up and say, *there, there they were*, you cannot know. People travel, from London to Sussex, to those seaside towns along the coast. Popular destinations for rest and recuperation. So one summer in 1905, and then in 1906, a set of people from Somers Town, behind St Pancras and the old church, took a train from Victoria or Waterloo to the seaside. A straight line down from the city, but no, the line is never straight; it wiggles, and it wanders; it dances about, and the girls on the train do the same.

History is like this: it jigs, and it spins and turns on a reel, and the things you remember move from pillar to post; from promenade and pier to harbour wall and bridge. They jump, they flicker, they spin and reel from one place to another. Time is unreliable; it moves fast and slow. So the painter who is out today – *the weather would be fine, they said* – must follow a steadier line. 'I follow a slow line,' says the painter. Three lines, two people and a bridge until they form a triangle: the girls in white on the other side of the harbour and the white tower. I see the people, but they are small and insignificant. What matters is the sky and the sea, that pillar, tall and proud, the lighthouse. There is my picture. And I stand beneath the shadow of the bridge, and I see the sun crossing the sky, the gulls flying over. I see people moving around the white column looking up. We are all looking up at the sky.

And the painter watches the moving shapes, and he will remember them: they are seabirds and soon they will fly off, back to their mother, the woman who waits for them along the pier.

The poet Stevie Smith wouldn't have stayed longer than a week in Littlehampton. The wind was too biting, the fish too salty, and the locals *a little too local*, she complained to her old aunt in one of her letters home. But Stevie had a friend who lived off the common. Mr Hargreaves, or Patrick as he was known to her in the evenings, wasn't exactly a fan – Miss Smith already had many of those – but he was one of the rarer things in her life, an old flame. Miss Smith had kissed Patrick, or rather, he had kissed her, one night near another old bandstand in Bermondsey.

They had known each other from church; he was a regular attender, and Stevie, whose real name was Florence, was very fond of this man from the church. He called her Margaret, or

Meg, but in latter years it had descended into Peggie, depending on what mood he was in. Mr Hargreaves enjoyed creating monikers for everyone. Patrick Hargreaves had one of those crosswordy minds that enjoys rearranging letters to suit riddles and clues. Peggie thought it very silly and sat around with her novel. Every summer she reread her favourite Victorians because, she said, they were too gloomy for the winter months. Just now she was working her way through *Middlemarch*, as Mr Hargreaves sat with his pencil behind his ear frowning at his paper.

'Gosh, doesn't George Eliot write long sentences!'

'Mmm. Yes.'

'P, you're not listening. I just read you an exquisite line.'

'Line, Peg dear, or sentence? I thought you were a poet.'

'Oh, don't be such a pedant. One forgets how young Dorothea is . . . such a foolish girl. She *is* a foolish girl really, don't you think, P?'

'Mm.' Mr Hargreaves sat with his pencil paused and ready to strike. Stevie looked over at her companion: he wasn't listening. How did men get away with that while women always feel so ashamed when they ignore someone?

'I met a quaint old lady today. She was just like something from a nursery rhyme.'

'Mmm. Four across . . . omelette in French, plus frying pan.' Mr Hargreaves looked up. 'Quaint did you say? You think everyone is quaint.'

'That's just what I mean. She was like something from one of those Victorian nursery rhymes, all behatted and beribboned. Well, not exactly, but certainly hatted. Her name was Mary.'

'One of your ancestors, Peg? Now help me with this clue . . . Frying pan in French.'

'I've no idea, dear P.'

'*Frirer* is to fry. Let me see, *poêle à frire*, I think.'

'They didn't expect us to fry anything in a pan at North London Collegiate.'

'Very short-sighted of them.'

'*Oeuf en poêle à frire.* I'm not sure that's correct. *A la poêle . . .* sounds more like it.'

'I'm afraid I've lost you, P.'

'The art of frying an egg, Peg. It's a fine art.'

'Speaking of which, let's have eggs for supper.'

'Fried?'

'Why not. And a bit of bacon.'

'What were you saying about that old dame you met?'

'Oh, P, stop pretending you're interested. I said I'd go and hear her play the organ. She seemed keen.'

'All old ladies love an audience, Peg.'

'And all old gentlemen too.'

Mr and Mrs Davie
(The working folk)

MR DAVIE lived on Pier Road, in one of the houses with narrow steps; a devil to get in and out of with a pram. But he did, he and his wife too, both with flaming red hair to match their mood. A bundle of angry nerves with the baby screaming and a toddler in tow, caught in the spokes of the pram. A rickety old thing, you thought, as you passed by on your bike. Mr Davie, my English teacher, can't have much money, he's struggling. Struggling people have a certain look: unwashed hair, scuffed shoes, tissues trailing from their pockets. Struggling people fall down the stairs with toast in their hand and a pram that won't move. Mr Davie is distracted; he is struggling with *that dreadful new syllabus*. 'That's not literature,' Mum says, when I showed her the poems. 'Why on earth would a woman call herself *Stevie* unless to draw attention to herself?' Mr Davie likes Stevie Smith. He doesn't think she's dreadful.

I liked Stevie Smith because she sounded serious and silly all at once. Then, I wasn't sure if it was poetry, but now I know it was. Poetry never tells you exactly what's going on. Never speaks the whole truth. You have to find the rest. There are always faint lines, something half seen or heard, like the words you hum under your breath. Mrs Plover crossing the kitchen to put the kettle on, thinking about her Harold and how he went.

'Harold, are you asleep, Harold, I remember your leap.' It goes like that, the poem by Stevie Smith about a man called Harold who took a brave leap across *two promontories*. A promontory is a cliff, poor Harold. He fell into the sea and the sea smothered him. It might have been an accident, you never know.

People do like to talk. I wonder what Cyril thought. Probably too polite to ask, Uncle Cyril, if that's who he was, the man in Mrs Plover's kitchen. If it *was* Uncle Cyril, then he's simpler than I thought. Poor Cyril, and poor Mrs Plover. She knows he will never come back, her atheling-born. Harold was grander than she. He knew some Latin and Greek; he had friends in high places. Her people were lower: thatchers and farmers and grocers, men with grubby hands. It was Harold who taught her poetry – Hilda sighs and puts down her peeler – a man with a kindly face is peering through the window. He is lifting his hands to the glass and showing his nails, black tips, filthy.

He did that when he was ready for his tea, then he would come in and sit by the fire and talk. Talk about all the village people, the people of Lyminster and Wick and Littlehampton and what they knew and didn't know. Harold knew everyone. He knew that lady called Mary, the sort that associated with grand sorts. Lady this and Lady that, Hilda can't quite remember, but I think one of them was an Emmeline, which would make a nice name for a cow or a cat. *What do you think? Cyril? Cyril? Are you there?*

I think Cyril would like Stevie Smith for the cats; she writes about cats. I like that. She writes about being lonely. Isn't everyone? About death and drowning, mud and *loamishness*, which is to say: 'It's a bit lonely stuck down here in the mud with my old shoes on. Lend us a hand up, won't you?' I reckon that's why Mr Davie liked Stevie – Mr Davie calls her Stevie – I like that.

Mr Davie has holes in his shoes, he's struggling; and so are the people in Stevie Smith's poems. People who don't like their children; people going to church to sing hymns, although they don't believe in God, and they put no money in the collection purse. People who like their history, ancient and old and classical, their Shakespeare and their Tennyson, their Greek tragedy. She's a proper poet really, because those are poet-y sorts of things, and Mr Davie likes her because she's a poet-y sort of person.

Mr Davie, whose name *might be* Francis, is married to a poet or a singer, but Mrs Davie has to pull pints at the Anchor to keep the wolf from the door. Mr Davie is a communist or a socialist, I can't remember which, but I think it's good to be both; you should definitely *try* to be both. But Mr Davie has *betrayed his principles*. 'It's no life at all, this sort of life, working for a head-mistress in a private school on Saturdays, the one day of the week I should have off,' he says to us one day just before the bell rings – and so Mr Davie is struggling.

Sometimes he runs a poetry competition, and we compete for a £5 note. This leads to All Sorts of Dreadful Attempts. A Dreadful Attempt is when someone has failed to assail the Great Wall of Poetry. That's all of us, except William Shakespeare, William Blake, William Wordsworth, Lord Alfred Tennyson and perhaps Stevie Smith, but we're not quite sure about her, we're still deciding.

Stevie writes about cats and money. Death, money, marriage, houses and homes, which comes back to how much you have stashed at the bank. Mr Davie keeps change in his pocket for the slot machines. He goes to the funfair after the sun goes down and tries his luck on the fruit machines. Mr Davie always has change in his pockets. I can hear it bouncing while he writes on the blackboard. His pockets jangle, and his wife, when she hears, starts to nark.

Where are the notes, where are the notes, Francis, the notes?

Without notes there'll be no rent and I'll have to take an extra shift at the Anchor. She calculates, Caitlin Davie is always calculating, her brain is fried by calculating. She needs more milk for the baby. The dried stuff is expensive, and the school only want Francis on Mondays, Tuesdays and Thursdays. That isn't a proper job. Caitlin shakes her head, tugs at the hand of the infant and drags her down the steps.

The child begins to bawl; the wind is cold; she doesn't want to go out. What child in their right mind would want to go out today, what mother either? She's tired, and the wind makes her more so: there wasn't enough sleep last night; there is never enough sleep because the child is always waking. She's waking now, her mouth open, rarely shut, always open, always wanting more. Sometimes Caitlin wants to whack it closed – but you didn't do that – a good mother never did that. *It won't do, it won't do, it won't do, Caitlin Davie!* Nothing will ever do, not even the silk sheets they were given for their wedding. *Who needs feckin' silk sheets when you can't sleep?*

Not Waving but Drowning
(A postcard)

POSTCARDS NEVER TELL the truth. Always there is the too-blue sky and the white-crested waves. Always the sun is high in the sky, so bright it is dazzling, as though someone has drawn it on for the occasion. Always the people on the beach look lazy and happy, as though this were heaven or the Holy Land. As though they were pilgrims from grimy-city spaces come to wash off their filth. As though they were expecting the sea to stretch out their worn muscles, bind up their wounds and remake them. As though they knew the beach and the sea better than we did, the direction and force of the wind, her crossness. Because the people in the pretty postcards always look as though they are there to make the place look smarter. But the sea is never pretty, though she is smart, and the wind is always sharp and fierce; and the brambles on the gorse bush sprawling over the sea wall will hurt if you touch her. She is yellow, but she will soon turn you red.

It happened like this: I went out too far beyond the breakwater. Maze always said, don't go out too far, she will get you, the furious monster with her white teeth. Christ will not walk out on the water to fetch you; such miracles do not occur. *Just mind yourself. Watch how you go! Beware!*

It happens like this: on the shore there are two girls playing with a ball. Their hair barely moves, their brown limbs shine with sun and sand. It's hard not to notice them, your beach friends. They are not like the other children on the beach, mangier and more disgraceful. They play nicely together, and the ball goes back and forth. Then the man with a large belly walks by and smiles; he waves gently, and one girl turns her head. Valerie, older than her years. She notices you out there bobbing on the waves, being where you have no business being, waving back at her. At the beach, at the fat man, at thin little Natalie, her sister, in her white beach dress. You, bobbing on the waves so happy to be in reach of friends. Far out, far beyond, as though your life depended on it: this space, and you, showing off to your new friends.

How brave you are, how strong, how they admire you, the people on the shore. They say, how lovely to see children swimming so freely. What a delightful summer we are having, so fortunate with the weather. It's been three weeks now, not a cloud in the sky, do you come down most days? And the sun continues to shine, heating up the pebbles, so that the people just arriving feel the scorch on their skin. Feet burn easily, did anyone bring the towels?

The sun has been out every day and you have been to the beach with your beach friends. You have made sandcastles together. You have collected shells. You have swum out together. Your friends have made you brave, and now you are alone, your arm sinking beneath the foam. Natalie and Valerie can swim like fish. You can too. Whatever they can do you can do better.

In your crochet bikini into the water where the waves are white and foamy, and your costume is full of holes. That's to let the air in, your mother says, but the water fills the holes, your ears, your mouth, your nose. You cannot breathe, though you have been told swimming is as natural as breathing. Good posture, keep your head up, your shoulders back, like a butterfly. See how she flits and flies, so easily. The sea will lift you safe to shore.

But something is wrong: you cannot lift your head; a great weight is pulling it down. A huge white pillow covers your face, you cannot see the sky, the monster's face is white and terrible.

On the shore Valerie's face begins to pucker; something is wrong, you have been out too long. Her arms flex with concern; she strides up and down.

Her sister throws the ball, but she does not catch it. 'Val, watch out. Here, catch!' But Valerie does not catch the ball. She strides out towards the shore. Now she is in the water, she is plunging in. Over her shoulders the cold sea goes and seals her in. Valerie is inside the water. She strides with her arms, with her legs.

Valerie is a fish, she is a merman, she is half boy, half man. She bears the brunt of the waves. She sees your head bobbing; it is a sinking float, a tiny dinghy with no air, a punctured beach ball. Beach balls go pop, plastic shreds fly everywhere. Hit the ball with the back of your wrist, punch it with your strong bones, it will soon come up for air.

Valerie's bones are strong. She drank much milk as a child. She was fed buttery bread and butter. She is strong, even beneath the waves. Thirteen this summer, an extra inch along her arms to haul you in with. Valerie has your head. It is deadweight and your eyes are closed. Your mouth is open, your eyes too. You are a frightened fish, but Valerie is not frightened. She knows what to do; she grabs you by the belly and wraps her arms around you. You are her catch, her big sea bass. Valerie pulls you spluttering across the waves. Your mouth is full of water, your eyes staring at the sky.

The shore is here now, your legs are stumbling, Valerie pulls you up onto the shingle. It cuts your legs and thighs. 'Stand up,' says Valerie. 'Stand up.' Everyone is looking. They are alarmed, the people on the beach, who have come down for the day to play. Natalie drops her beach ball; your mouth is hanging, you are a floppy fish.

'Did you drown?' asks Natalie. 'Were you drowning?'

'She didn't drown, Nat.'

You gasp and the water comes spouting out. Fish don't spout water, you are not a fish, but Valerie is a silvery fish drying in the sun. She picks up the ball and throws it towards her sister. 'Here, catch.' The man with the large belly slides by. He smiles. The children are happy. They play ball on the beach, and the man lifts his hand and waves. He likes children. He comes down to the sea to see them. Their skin is delicious like bacon.

Children remain a mystery to those they have sprung from. The door to the womb closes and forever after we remain separate. Mary knew this aged twelve; she knew it more aged twenty. Mother will always care more about hats and ribbons and the colour of her cheeks against pale silk. Children are hard on their parents. When you grow up you can make any sort of friends you prefer. You can dare to wander anywhere.

And Mary did. She made friends with Emmeline Pethick-Lawrence and Lady Constance Georgina Lytton, both ladies born and bred, so Mother can't be too dissatisfied with that. But Mother always found something to criticise, so when Mary moved in with Emmeline, Mother was full of frowns and woes. 'And would you believe it? Lady Constance has moved in round the corner, in a poky little flat no doubt? What on earth are they doing in such places?'

'We live among the poor,' says Mary. 'But let's not call them that, they are the working folk.'

Mr Pitman

At some point in her life my grandmother lived in a small flat off a poky alleyway. I didn't know she had a flat until she began giving me typing lessons – then the flat suddenly appeared – on Saturday mornings when I was eight, at eleven o'clock in the morning.

The flat was at the end of the alleyway and the alleyway was dark and dank and smelled of men. Men lived on the other side of the darkness and came stumbling out through a battered door, dribbling and drooling, and holding silver cans. But we went through the white door opposite, and it was a world of furry plants and flowers. Soft geranium leaves and prickly cacti and crinkly skin. White talcum powder flying through the air, and everything taking much longer: the world on hands and knees.

Maze had arthritis and it took her a long time to climb the stairs. Arthritis slows you down, and if you have shopping you go even slower. One step at a time, lifting the bag in front of you.

'As heavy as a wee small thing,' said Maze. *Puff*. Here we are! Those stairs nearly do me in. Whose idea was that, to put stairs in here?' And then I hated the stairs for making my grandmother older.

But the Maze who taught me typing was not so old; in her sixties perhaps, retired. I don't know how old exactly because *retirement* was just a word, and I wasn't sure what it meant. Only that she stopped cycling her bicycle along the seafront to a place called the Zachary Merton where she cleaned up the sticky mess of children being born. Where she changed beds and wiped down floors, emptied buckets and potties and bedpans and bent forwards and backwards all day long.

Once Maze had had another life, and in that life, she sat at a desk on an office chair and typed sixty words a minute. Mr Pitman's typing course taught her how to type fast enough to find herself a job. Once, a long time ago, my grandmother had sat on a chair at a desk and been paid to type. She did everything Mr Pitman told her to do.

Mr Pitman, a man with black hair greying at the roots, slicked back with oil. A pale man pacing the classroom at the top of the factory building in Shoreham-by-Sea. Maze was twenty-two and she did whatever Mr Pitman said because he was a bit of a sergeant major and liked to march up and down with a ruler slapping the desk as he dictated.

When he did, the dust jumped, and Edna May jumped too, and she kicked over her handbag and yelped like a small dog. Then Mr Pitman frowned down upon her bag and said, 'What's that doing there? Put it under your desk!' Then he stared long and hard at Maze's shoes and ankles and legs. So Maze stared too to see what was wrong and wondered whether her stockings were the wrong colour. Eh hem! Type!

Mr Pitman rapped the desk with his ruler.

Mr Pitman rapped the desk with his wooden ruler.

Mr Pitman leaned heavily against the desk with his wooden ruler which bent back like a sapling.

As he leaned his full weight against his ruler, Mr Pitman sighed heavily and deeply in the way women do in old films when they are left alone in high winds in moody places.

Places where the trees bend backwards and lour against a dark sky, before a dark figure emerges from the back of the screen and glowers, and the camera moves across their sweaty face, and you wonder when was the last time they had a bath? Of course you would never think that of Mr Pitman because he was always so well dressed, so dapper, and carried a handkerchief in his breast pocket for wiping his brow.

Indeed, Mr Pitman sighed deeply and heavily as though he were a woman left alone in a wild, windswept spot in a moody barren place, like in that old black and white film of *Gone with the Wind*.

Her name is Scarlett, and she pouts.

Mr Pitman would recognise her sort immediately and shout, 'Sixty words a minute, my girl!' and come down hard on her with his ruler.

Mr Pitman liked his girls to type sixty words a minute, sixty to eighty, but it helped that I was afraid of him, and the big hands of the black clock ticking loudly above our heads: *forty seconds, ladies, thirty, twenty, ten, five seconds, ladies. Stop typing now!* Maze could hardly breathe; the clock was so loud it squeezed all the air out of the room and suddenly Mr Pitman's face was right in front of her, and his neck was craning up at the clock, and the room was filled with the heavy sound of hands frozen over keys. And then there was a gasp! *Clickety-clack-clack.* Someone in the room was still typing – and well, let me tell you, Mr Pitman did not like that – and he pointed with his wooden stick out the window towards the harbour.

'Pull yourself together, girl! People lose life and limb out at sea. That's why we must give generously to the Lifeboat Fund. Have you, young lady, given generously? Have you given to the Royal National Lifeboat Institute?'

'RNLI. Capitals, dear. Look down at the keys for now, dear, just while you're learning their place.' Real typists knew how to touch type, which meant you never looked at the keys, but straight ahead. At the top of the carriage where the ribbon was passing across – *Remington, Remington, Remington, here it comes! Remington – there she goes – your favourite filly – racing across the silver and white tabs, that hard shiny ruler measured in inches*: 1.0, 2.0, 3.0, 4.0. Count until you reach 8.0 across, then go back the other way and start again. 1.0, 2.0, 3.0, 4.0 . . . typing was like going to the races. You could barely keep up with the horse out front.

'You've gone too far, dear! Push the carriage over and start again!' *Ting-ting! Ting!* And my grandmother began to dictate.

'"Mr Barclay" – spelled like the bank with a capital B – "Mr Barclay asked Miss Timms" – two m's – "to bring him his cup of tea at eleven o'clock. Mr Barclay liked his tea with full fat milk, straight from the dairy, and Miss Timms went to fetch his milk from the grocer's three times a week."'

'There are too many names!'

'Well, most correspondence is filled with names, dear. Your spelling will have to be good too. People get very cross when their name is spelled wrong.'

'When are we having porridge?'

'When you've finished this sentence: "But one morning Miss Timms arrived and there was a notice on the door and a black bin bag over the window. Miss Timms looked very put out."'

'What happened? Were they closing down?'

'I'll tell you next time! Now let's have our porridge.'

'Had they run out of money? Did someone smash the window? Were the police called?'

'Poor Mr Barclay, without his milk. Now come and help stir the oats, they're thickening.'

Miss Cull

THERE WERE WOMEN who went into the world and earned a living. Some women did this, but what you don't see in your own life you can only imagine, and I did. Plenty of people live lives of work and busyness, plenty of people pay their rent. Even poets. Stevie Smith went out to work, Mr Davie said, sounding pleased. Private secretary to a big publisher, Sir Neville Pearson, what a ridiculous name. She typed her poems during the lunch hour. I don't know if I believed Mr Davie, because if you worked for a man called Sir Neville Pearson you'd have to spend most of your lunchtime practising typing up his name.

Miss Cull did, the spinster who lived in the flats opposite. She earned her living. What can I tell you of her? That she wore her blouse necks high and tight and her back ramrod straight. In the morning she carefully unfolds a thermal vest and pulls the sleeves gently; unties the ribbon around the neckline to make sure it isn't crumpled. Everything must be nice and smooth. She crosses her room, a very small room, twenty feet by twenty. It is a modestly sized flat, she tells the ladies at the church, a cosy little flat on the twelfth floor. KINGSMERE, I live in KINGSMERE, and everyone looks very impressed, because Kingsmere has only been there for a year or two.

'Built last spring,' says Miss Cull, looking very pleased. Miss Braithwaite is surely wondering where on earth the money came from for Miss Cull to be a *resident* of Kingsmere.

Miss Cull holds two small posts, because music is expensive and all we can afford is a choir and recorder club. 'So let's have lots of hymns,' Miss Cull said to Mr Maynard, the headmaster, when she came for her interview some years ago.

'Yes, of course, hymns are delicious . . . I mean, hymns are divine. "Onward Christian Soldiers"!' And Miss Cull smiled a watery smile. She could play the piano passably well, that was enough, surely?

Poor Miss Cull, no one had ever kissed her, that's what we all thought; because children can be two things at once: sweet and sour. And everyone at school said Miss Cull was a dried-up old spinster who no man would ever ask out, who no one would ever dream of taking to the Beach Hotel. There's a woman who speaks far too much of her cat, thought Miss Braithwaite. A lonely soul, Miss Cull, with her little white cat who sits on the windowsill looking down upon the people of Granville Road. I must have her in for tea next Sunday, I shall ask her after church. And Miss Braithwaite makes a mental note to feel sorry for Miss Cull.

But Miss Cull has her secrets like all of us; she has her spare room if you can call it that. Six feet by eight, or perhaps eight feet by eight, at most ten by ten. In truth, it's mainly wall. What's the difference between a room and a cupboard? Not much, I think. Here, Miss Cull keeps her hymn books stacked against the wall, covered in thick plastic to protect them from grubby hands. Every Sunday she cleans her hymn books with a hot, soapy sponge. Nice and thick, just like skin, she thinks, as she wipes back and front, front and back, and sets them out to dry on the floor.

On a warm day she takes her hymn books out to dry on the balcony. Lines them up against the sunny wall. Lizards drying in the sun. Then she goes back inside to her special chest of drawers. But the drawer is stuck, and Miss Cull is anxious. She is biting her teeth and pulling hard with both hands. POP! Her drawer flies open, and Miss Cull sees what she has longed to see. Shiny eyes and red lips, that small, cute nose. Strands of straight blonde hair. *Oh, poppet,* she says, *oh poppet!*

And I say, Miss Cull, *poppet* is an old word, and it was my mother's favourite for me, for all her children. It means 'girl' or 'doll', but which is it? You can't have both. Either you are a living thing or something made from raggedy clothes: an orphan stuffed away in a drawer. *Puppa,* poppet, puppet. Stand her up, let her dance on her strings – Miss Cull, let the child sing!

The Vanishing Lady

I REMEMBER A FILM about a lady vanishing. My grandmother loved it, and so we watched it over and over. Maze loved old films, anything in black and white, films where people spoke terribly polite. *How do they get anything done when they are all so, so terribly polite?* But still people complain, English people, the people travelling abroad; even the nice old lady due to catch the train in the morning along with everyone else. Yes, even she must call the concierge to stop the racket of singing and piping and dancing from the jolly locals. They are only having fun, and the old lady usually likes her bit of music; she loves a lovely tune, a serenade. She doesn't mind the man outside her window singing away, lilting and lilting, the old tunes – and my grandmother loves those too, 'The White Cliffs of Dover'. That old tune. How does it go? Maze sang it all the time.

There'll be bluebirds over the white cliffs of Dover, tomorrow, just wait and see, there'll be love and laughter and peace ever after, tomorrow when the world is free. Everyone in *The Lady Vanishes* wants something; even though they've just been on holiday, they still all want. Let me give you a précis. Miss Braithwaite would be

Bluebirds over the white cliffs of Dover

happy if I gave you a summary, a way of understanding the gist of the matter.

People, there are a set of them, are somewhere in the mountains: at a resort, a hostel, an inn, a hotel, a chalet somewhere in Austria or Germany or Switzerland. They are hotel guests and they speak some German; everyone speaks some German, including the old lady who tells the English gentlemen she meets on the train that carries the people away from the resort, that she loves the mountains like her own family. The mountains, she says, wear white hats, a Papa hat and a Mama hat and two smaller hats for the children; and this old lady hums and sings to herself and the gentlemen listening in the buffet car think she is full of whimsy, which means toys. The old lady has a bag of tricks, which is why she is so good with children. The gentlemen she travels with don't enjoy Austria or Germany or Switzerland because no one there plays cricket, and the food is bad, but the main point is the journey home. Everyone wants to catch the train home as soon as possible; they wish to resume life as it was before. To resume: to take back, to repossess, to find the courage, strength and hope to take back up again with the place where they left off. To restart what had begun, that old familiar plot.

The English gentlemen – there are two of them – are missing the cricket terribly. So they play cricket with the sugar cubes that come with their tea, until the old lady interrupts their game when she leans across the railway carriage and asks them politely, terribly politely, whether she might have the sugar, because her tea has come without it. Annoyed, they pass the old lady the sugar.

She is travelling with a young lady called Iris, Iris Henderson. Iris is going home to marry a man she doesn't love. But Iris has banged her head, and now no one believes her. No one believes she has seen what she says she has seen. That she saw the old lady who was travelling with her only a moment ago; the lady she took her tea with inside the buffet car; the little old lady she chattered happily away to, or as happily as you can when you have banged your head and begun to see the world strangely.

'What you need is a good, strong cup of tea. Now, come along.' And so they proceed to the buffet car, the old lady leading the young woman, the young woman following the old lady.

'I always think it's better to sit in the middle of the coach when it's shaking.' And indeed it was, the train was shaking horribly, and Iris Henderson's head was hurting horribly too.

'A pot of tea for two, now make sure the water is absolutely boiling,' the old lady says to the waiter. 'And please make sure they make it from this.' And she hands over a packet of tea to the waiter. 'I don't drink anything else, and neither do my mother and father, who are in excellent health, and I like to follow in their footsteps.' Iris Henderson listens to the old lady chatter away and leans forward across the table.

'I don't believe we've been introduced. My name is Iris Henderson and I'm going home to be married.'

'How very exciting, I do hope you'll be happy,' says the older lady to her young companion, and 'I do hope you will have children; I always think having children around me for so many years has kept me young for my age – don't you think?' she asks her younger companion – who can hardly say no. And then the older lady begins to tell the younger one her name, but the train whistle screams and screeches, so she writes her name upon the window through the condensation – 'F-R-O-Y' – as the train crosses an old Roman viaduct so wide it takes up the entire screen.

Over it goes, the train, clickety-clack, shaking and shaking from side to side, so that Iris Henderson begins to nod off. And the younger lady closes her eyes and falls asleep and the train whips along, and then sometime later the whistle blows loudly, and she wakes up to find that her friend is no longer in the seat in front of her.

'Have you seen my friend? The English lady, where is she?' And the severe-looking Austrian or German or Swiss couple sitting opposite say, 'There has been no English lady here.' So Iris becomes terribly upset and begins to ask everyone about the little English lady she was travelling with just a while ago. The lady who handed the waiter in the dining car the special packet of tea. 'But she gave you a special packet of tea, you must remember that?' And then the waiter in the car tells her that only *she* had taken tea, that only one lady paid for the tea, and he shows her the bill.

'I suppose you haven't seen my friend?' Iris keeps asking.

And what was she wearing? they all ask.

And Iris says: 'Tweed, oatmeal flecked with brown, three quarter coat with patched pockets, a scarf, a felt hat, brown shoes, a turtle shirt, a small blue handkerchief in her breast pocket. The middle-aged ordinary little English woman who sat just opposite me a moment ago. Where is she?'

We watched the film over and over, it's that sort of film, and I learned some of the words off by heart because I wanted to hear what it was the old lady was saying as the train screamed through the tunnel. But I couldn't hear her, *I couldn't hear her!* And still, all the way through that long and ugly scream, Iris Henderson remained polite, as she leaned in to say, 'I'm sorry I can't hear, what did you say?' Until the old lady understood she couldn't hear and turned towards the window and began to write on the glass with her finger. Her name.

Sometimes I wake up in the night still and wonder where that old lady has got to. 'F-R-O-Y, it rhymes with JOY,' she says to Iris, just as the tea arrives on the buffet car table and the old lady turns to smile at the waiter. She was always smiling, warmly, blithely, kindly; even through the long screech of the train.

Sally Green

My mother had a friend at Worthing High School, her name was Sally Green, and she came top of the county in Latin, and everyone thought, What a dream! Sally went on to study at Oxford University, and my mother loved her for that. All her life Angela hankered after Sally and her Latin declensions, her *by*, *with*, *to* and *from*, her careful sense of timing. Sally Green from Worthing High who was going up to Oxford with so many farewell smiles.

Sally, who got on a train at Shoreham-by-Sea with a plaid suitcase and went to London. Where she changed from Victoria to Paddington, before taking the northwest line towards the city of dreaming spires. Sally, who went to a college where they took only women named after a Lady that stood on the banks of the River Cherwell where there were summer parties. Sally, the girl, shy and bespectacled from Sompting, which is near Lancing, which is near Worthing, off the A259, the main road that runs through the Downs. You can see the old church from there; it has a Saxon tower, although some say Norman, but they are ignorant of their history. Saxon towers are short and squat; the Normans preferred lofty spires, their gods must have been taller – but there were none at that college – where the girl called Sally, shy and bespectacled, tried to make conversation. About Cicero and his excellent use of logic, his legal syntax, and she dreamed of learning like him, she told the old don in front of her; because Cicero had been a good lawyer, and if you understood the rules of logic and grammar, the right declensions, the apposite nouns, you *could go and work in the city*, her tutor said – *there will always be work for legal secretaries* – and the girl with mousy hair pushed her glasses further up her nose as she always did when she didn't know the answer.

The Photograph
'Sally Green on the High, in 1966 (or 7?)'

A mousy girl in a scholar's gown, hair falling over her face, the corner of her collar turned up because it is a warm day in June and her friend has come up to visit from Sussex. Angela has come up on the train to see Sally Green. Dear Angela, Lovely Angela, they are looking at *you*, not Sally. Angela who grips the small black box and clicks, Angela who must take some photographs because she promised Mother and she promised Father and she promised the Woman Next Door. So many promises, and how do you know if you're taking a good one? She clicks. The University Church of St Mary's, her friend said, the church on the High, that's where we are: staring at the spire, our necks craned at an angle, look Ange! *Click*. And behind us this lovely tree which has stood here for years, lending its shape to the High Street. So many photographs

Angela grips the small black box

and clicks

of this cherry, so many smiles beneath the blossom, so many visitors passing by on that warm June day stopping to look at the pretty girl beneath the cherry tree. They shuffle by, she clicks.

'Do you have a good one, yet?'

Sally is keen. It is hot. Her face is damp. Sally would like to take her friend to the riverbank. The Cherwell, where they will arrange themselves. Two girls discussing their plans, their legs laid out. Ange will take off her nylons, Sally will kick off her shoes, small and flat with laces, brogues. From Aunty Phyllis, for Oxford, *how exciting, Sally!* Two girls discussing their plans. But Ange has none – she will go home and lengthen the hem of her summer dress – and Sally, Sally is thinking of her essay. Two lives, two sides of the riverbank. Sally is pointing west, across the bridge leading from the university park where they are sprawled. *Marston, there is a pretty village there.* It is too hot to move, says Ange. Let's stay here. They close their eyes, they sleep.

It is hot, and Angela starts to hear a tune; she is prone to hearing tunes, it is a nervous habit. *Mary, Mary, quite contrary, how does your garden grow?* She begins to drift off, it is hot, and her head is aching, and she has been clicking for so long now with this black box she hardly knows where she is. All she can hear is that tune, all she can see are those drawings from Old Mother Goose.

Old Maids

'What does all this experience mean? Whither does it lead?
What is the link between the child dreaming dreams and
seeing visions and the woman sitting in judgment on her
fellows on the Magistrates Bench?'
(Mary Neal, 'A Tale Told', an unpublished autobiography)

Miss cull is tending to the church garden. She has a penchant for planting bulbs. Edith likes the feeling of burying something deep down. 'Not too deep, Edith dear,' Mary says. 'Three or four inches is quite enough. We're not burying bodies.'

After Mary leaves – Edith is relieved – she digs further, on her hands and knees. It is satisfying to feel the crunch of stones against her trowel; it is satisfying this garden worship. Here you are, Edith, turning over the Lord's soil. Now lift your knees!

Edith is planting narcissi, paper whites to be precise, along the church path. They may not come up, but she'd like to try, this is no reason why not: now is the season for planting out. It is the end of the summer, and the cool winds have set in. She sees a white parade of floppy handkerchiefs greeting her, everyone waving. She begins to plant furiously.

White heads bobbing up and down the path. Pointy way up, Edith, pointy way up, let's see the crown! The bulbs come thick and fast, they are pressed too much together, but Edith would like a nice crowd waving.

'She has no garden of her own, so naturally she likes to do her part,' says Miss Braithwaite to the vicar's wife as they sit inside the manse sipping tea. 'We all like to play our part, Greta, it's only natural.' Greta lowered her head and sipped her tea just a little louder than usual. She wanted to cover her thoughts; they are not charitable.

'I suppose she gets lonely in that flat, all the way up there. I wouldn't like it. I'd get giddy, wouldn't you? And all those seagulls cawing away. Seagulls get fatter, it seems, the higher you go.'

Miss Cull is planting furiously now; the soil is smooth and yielding, she has made it so. She tosses out the dry stones, pours in a drop of water, mixes it in, then plop, down she goes. There is a recipe to this, and she has it off by heart. But wait, Miss Cull begins to lose her bearings; she is wandering off track, and now the green verge is zig-zagging all around her. Miss Cull looks up and sees a white carpet; confetti strewn across the path. *Oh, how blessed are the children of the Lord!* She crawls on her hands and knees to the other side of the verge. I must cover this side too; all sides must be covered in white; all sides must be blessed. *And then the angel of the Lord appeared unto him in a flame of fire out of the midst of a bush.* But where was the bush, where was the sacred bush? The churchyard has turned it blue.

'Ceanothus, Greta. We must trim back the ceanothus.'

'I can do that tomorrow with the clippers.'

'Are they sharp enough, Greta?'

Miss Cull begins to feel anxious. She lowers her body and crawls. *I must find the bush, the burning bush, I must find my way to Israel!* There is a sharp scratch, a soft tear, her tights are beginning to go. *I must shed my skin*, and Miss Cull crawls until she can go no further, to the edge of the churchyard wall.

Young girls are waiting to be old maids. Angela thinks that this is what all her teachers think. We are young girls waiting to turn into old maids. In ten or twenty years from now we shall be discarded from the pack, like the Queen of Spades in that game we played.

Mary, Mary, quite contrary
How does your garden grow?
With silver bells, and cockle shells,
And cowslips all in a row.

Somehow there is always an old tune vexing her. Perhaps if she draws it out it will stop. 'I like to draw cottages,' she tells Miss Haines, her art teacher. 'They remind me of people wearing funny hats. I like chimney stacks. One day I will share a cottage with my friend Sally in Old Cokeham or Beeding or Bramber and we will put flowers in the windowsill and wear hats.' Angela begins to doodle.

Doodles

Cowslips tall her pensioners be
and cowslips grow on the Downs
above Cokeham village
where Sally lives.

Sally has a garden at the front
of
the pretty cottage where she lives
with her parents.
Her father is a minister
and his church is Saint Mary's
of
the Blessed Virgin
and she stands on the edge
of
Sompting Village where
      the rooks crow loudly
            through the beech trees

      where some nights the thrush beats
            through the gloaming,
                  as the minister says his prayers

as her pencil begins to soften
as the candle begins to burn
as the smoke rises from
the chimney

as she realises
a cottage is ideal for visitors
and home birds
who prefer to nest,
underneath the eaves.
We shall be homebirds,
We shall be cooing doves
     she sings.

Sally will make the trip into the city: and Angela will stay at home and tend to the garden: put on the wash, whiten the cuffs.

And when Sally comes home, she will teach Angela things: prepositions and conjunctions, all that business of belonging to someone, or being with someone other than yourself: all that reaching for a place over the hills and far away.

PART FOUR

A True Anon

The Last Train Home

AND LO AND BEHOLD, the photograph of Sally was never found; it vanished into that sticky summer air. I wonder whether my mother fudged all those shots because she felt uncomfortable being there, so that when she took the photographs to the man behind the counter all he could say was 'There's nothing here, love', and her heart fell to the floor.

'They're not very reliable, love,' he said when he saw her face. 'Not those little Kodak Brownies. You need something better if you want a good shot. This one has a fancy lens. That'll do the job.'

And she vowed she'd try harder next time. But there was no next time.

'It's time to catch the train, quick, Ange, run!'

Sally never called her Ange, how strange, but they managed it, they made it, and the young woman flung herself onto the last train home. Here she is. Dragging herself along the corridor, flopping inside an empty carriage, throwing open the window and settling into the corner. Her feet ache, her shoes pinch; she kicks them off and closes her eyes; her body tips and sways. *I'm a little teapot*, she can hear her mother singing, *I'm a little teapot short and stout*. She can see her sister, she can see herself, practising their tipping in the bathroom, out upon the front lawn. 'More space here,' says her mother. 'Now tip me over and pour me out.' And the young woman tips across her seat.

The train pulls into a station: an old lady climbs in. The step up is wide, but someone helps her. There is always someone kind. She finds a carriage with a young woman sleeping. The old lady stores her case on the rack above and settles in.

She tells the young woman that she has just come from a very hectic time as a governess, or was it a nanny, those distinctions are important. Certainly, she was never an au pair; in any case, she oversaw two precocious children, both girls, without a mother, only the father remained. A nice man, nice manners, nicely spoken, the children too, although they ran wild. She likes children but they are exhausting, and when they're not your own it takes more effort to make them pay heed. Of course, she's firm, very firm, children like that. They like to know where they stand; they like you more for it in the end. There's no point being too soft, you'll regret it. Children soon work out who is toffee and who is fudge. Sometimes it's hard to know what you can and can't say. You have to imagine what their mother would want, the mother who is never there. You become a sort of mother, that's what you are really, a second mother, and it can get quite awkward, especially with the father.

Of course, you don't have quite the same feelings, but you have some feelings, nonetheless. Feeling is the main thing, or *affection* you might say. It's difficult to conceal feelings with children. You'd like them to listen more, and they do, most of the time, but it's the father they pay most heed to, and he only appears every now and then. Spends most of his time in London. He has a flat there, off Piccadilly, and stays several times a week, usually Monday to Thursday, but sometimes Friday too. The week does seem very long without any adult company. I look forward to him coming through the door and I always take his hat for him. There's a hat stand right in the hallway, one of those lovely old Victorian ones. Looks just like a miniature tree, quite charming. I make sure there's nothing in the way when he comes through the door, not even the children; only me and the hat stand – and then a nice whisky and soda. Poor man, that job does take its toll . . .

People can talk forever. How long do we have? The journey between Oxford and Paddington is one hour. You can say a lot in an hour, you can tell your whole life. And so the train keeps jogging along and the old lady keeps moving too. She regrets not having children of her own, but the freedom is something she relishes. If you can call living in other people's houses freedom. It is a freedom of sorts. Your bills are covered and your meals. The hardest part is the affection; there is so much of it over the years, where do you put it all? You can only manage two decent-sized cases, and after a while they get quite battered, pulling them in and out of other people's houses, up and down the stairs.

Each time it's a different house, a different family, a different set of rules, you have to start again. Every family has its own tics, yours too, dear. What do your parents do, dear? No, let me guess. Your father's a solicitor; your mother a housewife, and a mother of course. I expect she's shy, just like you. Shyness is a lovely quality if it doesn't get in the way of you getting on in the world. Is he terribly strict, your father? Their bark is often worse than their bite. My father was like that, a proud man. Proud men want you to know that everything they have they made themselves. Nothing was handed to them on a plate. My father owned a button factory, it made him a fortune.

And the old lady keeps talking, and the train whistles through the tunnel, and the young woman continues to sleep, because she's had a terribly long day and it was very hot under that tree. And out on the water she felt very swoony. Was it the Cherwell, the Isis, the Thames? Sally said there were two rivers that meet, as in Mesopotamia, or is it Egypt? Two mighty rivers, the Tigris . . . and the Tiger . . . or is it the Nile? The train rolls along and the young woman sleeps. She sleeps and sleeps, and when the train rolls into the station, with a sudden jog, the old lady is no longer there. She has gone.

Angela

Carpe Diem. Seize the Day. You won't get a second chance. Opportunities come around only once. This is why Sally went away. And spring turned to summer, and the willows blossomed, and the roses, so carefully pruned last year, came out for the summer party. And the dons and their wives came out too upon the lawn and showered their praise upon the best and brightest: and Sally was among them, and Sally stayed among them and became one of the fold turning over her thoughts in hushed and hallowed libraries. How the Greeks won the war against the Spartans – with might and vanquish and a great deal of rhetoric – Sally learned it all.

And the roses fell and scattered, and the autumn winds moved in, and the young woman known as Ange had begun to make clothes for a living – and then maps – for the two, she said to the man in the government office, are related. Yes, maps are similar to dress patterns, all those shapes and lines. And she looks at her shoes.

And the roses fell and scattered

Black patent today, the pair she's always had, with a nice little strap running across. She hopes they don't show off her nylons too much because he's been staring at her leg for some time. Strange how men never seem interested in what an attractive girl has to say. Girl or woman, woman or girl, when does a woman begin? When she grows tall. Five foot seven or eight and then a lovely bit of lift in her hair. Blonde curls, full and round. When she was young, they fell like sausage curls down her back. Now they lift towards the heavens, and she has to set them with lacquer. Sometimes she adds a sash bow. Hair like hers never stays still, but what is the man with the bald head saying? He is wheezing, he is reaching for the tissue box. The girl is watching, she is always watching, because men must be watched. Spittle flies over and lands on her knee. She watches it slide down her leg as the man delivers his instructions on the job.

The job: to draw up maps of county boundaries; she must copy them out carefully. Replicate. Pay special attention to the coastline because the coastline is the boundary, the beginning and the end of watery space. Fishermen want to know where the coast begins and ends, where the murky rocks lie, the sharp teeth of the sea. We don't want any nasty accidents coming in or out of the harbour. The man behind the desk is beginning to sound irate.

So there is the job: how many boats in each harbour, how many bays to dock a boat, where the sand begins and ends, the nature of the terrain, rough or smooth. Copy out the maps and add any further details. There are old maps, your job is to update them, but we prefer that most things stay the same. We don't have the budget. Better if you keep things as they are, give or take a few details. A seamstress, you say? Then you must be good with your hands. What does a seamstress do? She explained, but the man was not looking at her hands.

She watches his mouth. Thin and grey, it flicks from side to side. A fish moving through shallow waters. Small specks of bread float on the surface – the tide is low – in a few hours it will come in and the pub on the quay will be open and he will go down and order a cold beer.

Meanwhile, there is this young woman in front of him with her lovely full legs, seems just the right sort. Will no doubt provide the right sort of statistics given a bit of a steer: 36-26-36.

Mum could have told you the best way to Dover. At some point she'd been given the job of mapping local districts, although what exactly she mapped was never clear. Mum was hired by the local government to draw the exits and entrances: where the sea met the land, the estuary, the harbour mouth. 'Think of it like a stage,' said the man in the local office. 'Were you ever on stage, Miss? You're pretty enough to act.'

She got the job, she said, because she'd been a seamstress and understood material; the weight of it, and how much slack was required to make it sit well. How materials fit together; the shape of things. Material breaks at some point, under duress, so you must give it slack. Everything that is made needs slack, space and distance. *Keep your distance*, she was always saying about the rough end of town. *Don't wander home that way. Take the other way.* So I did. I crossed over the river from East to West sands with my notebook and wrote down all the words we'd learned at school about the land around us: *incline, erosion, attrition, valley, escarpment, pervious, impervious, clay, chalk, limestone, hills, harbour, gradient, inlet, estuary, coastline, lagoon.* We don't have one of those around here. You'll have to go to Brighton for that, we tell

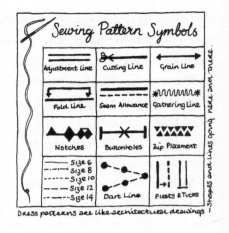

Dress patterns are like architectural drawings

the tourists. We have an oyster pond looking out across the harbour wall, and next to the rickety pier a set of women I've never seen before are parading about. People like to parade around the pond. Once it was for boating. Ladies in wide hats went out and pulled hard on their oars. But the women are not on boats, they are standing next to the harbour wall. One lone figure standing by herself, tall and square-jawed, looking up at the lighthouse. Poor unblinking thing. People have petitioned, I wonder if this lady is a petitioner too. Over her head seagulls are screeching. I look up, she looks up too. Its light hasn't blinked for years, and no one has replaced the bulb. This is what happens if you leave the council to manage your affairs. The figure nods her head gently. She knows. If you want anything done yourself you have to form your own committee, take charge, make your own plans. Follow your own vision, draw up your own maps. She's met someone who knows how to draw maps: a young woman with fair hair who lives on the other side of the pond. Past the old hotel, off the main road. Fair hair piled high, looks like an angel.

Mr Bald

MAPPING MEANT she'd had to swear to the Official Secrets Act, so they sent a man to follow her around the backstreets of Worthing to the little tearoom where she took her tea after work, the Copper Kettle, behind the cinema. As he approached he asked to see her handbag. What a cheek, she thought. But she lifted the leather straps from the floor and passed it over to the man with the solemn face who took it without a word.

Ange was proud of her bag; she'd spent all her savings on it. Deep blue, the colour of cornflowers, the satin lining. Satin flowed along the bottom of her bag – she loved the feel on her fingers – and now that man had his grubby hands in it. Keys, cough sweets, tissues, nothing wrong with that. Sherbet lemons, a packet of dress patterns, her black cotton gloves. Nothing wrong with that either. *There's nothing wrong with a lady carrying a nice bag.* Black leather, on sale at Bentalls, the last one in stock. She saved a year for it; on bad days it carried her through. Sometimes she sat in the office and played with it while the bald man was out. Opened and

Snap, the brass clips went on the bag,
Snap-snap-snap

closed it, opened and closed it until she felt calmer. Snap, the brass clips went, snap-snap-snap; and Mr Wentworth, the bald man, heard them as he pulled himself back up the stairs. What an aggravating sound, he thought. Now, I want my coffee!

'My coffee please, with cream! It's not too much to ask to keep a pot of cream in, is it?'

Did he call her Angela or Miss Bayley? Miss Bayley to assert himself, Angela to win her over. Usually it was Miss Bayley. She was young, eighteen or nineteen. At nineteen you are still a schoolgirl, but that's what he wanted. A girl to say please and thank you and would you like your coffee, Mr Wentworth? I've got your cream – but today she hadn't, she'd forgotten. Lost herself inside a dream.

She was thinking of Sally waving goodbye at the station, her face turning blurry as she turned one final time to wave, as Angela begins to fumble with her bag. 'Where have I put it, where have I put it, where have I put it?' For years she asked herself that question. *Where was her photograph of Sally Green?* If only she could find the photograph of Sally, things might have gone differently for Ange. As the years passed, the image of Sally began to fade: a pale-faced girl with mousy hair lifting her hand to wave. Even the wave began to fade. All that was left was her bag. Black patent leather, shiny and waxy as a turtle.

She liked to pet it; several times a day she reached down for it or felt it with her toes. Her bag was her docking bay, her harbour, her satin sea. Once she made the mistake of putting Mr W's cream inside it and the lid split, leaving a couple of thick cream spots on the lining. That contamination was a sign of her failure. All afternoon she rubbed and rubbed at it with cold water, then warm, then hot. She left it to dry on the windowsill and in between her letters went to check on it: the spots were paler than before. Spots were a sign of ill-health – her bag had become poorly – she thought about tearing out the lining and adding a new one. Too much work, and she might not be able to feed it back in; the shape was difficult, an oblong, not a square. Perhaps she could tear out a part, lay over a new section, start again. *Oh, that damn cream!*

The next day she forgot it – she'd not forgotten before – and he was cross. *She wouldn't do it again, there was still time to go. She would go now and be back in a jiffy. I'll run!* She grabbed her bag, the young woman with the blonde hair piled high.

Angela was an ordinary girl who happened to be beautiful, regal really. She just lacked the essential element; a confident girl would never have stuck the job with Mr Bald. She'd have left after the first week, the first month, after the first pay cheque. But Ange stuck it out. She typed the letters he wanted and took the minutes. When he asked her to go down to the harbour to count the number of fishing boats, she did. Then she typed up the minutes of the district meetings. Added to the agenda whatever it was Mr Bald wanted to push through. There was usually some dispute with another Mr Bald, and when that was the case, he asked Angela to underline certain words and sentences.

It was expressly agreed that the budget for Shoreham beach, including the bridge, but especially the bridge, will not be reviewed until after the next tax year.
(Underlined heavily)

Angela thought this looked rude, but no one ever asked her opinion. She just typed, copied up the lines on the map, added a few of her own. Was always careful – delicate and in pencil – always ready to erase. Careful to count the number of additions. 'We have a very limited budget, young lady. Think yourself lucky for what you're learning here.' She was learning that an HB pencil and an eraser were enough, a small notebook, and a good pair of legs. The district assigned to her was small. Mr Bald didn't want any changes. She learned to copy and add very little; nothing new, my girl. 'This is an historic place, my girl. Everything set out nicely already. We must think of the budget, we must not get ahead of ourselves.' Mr Bald slurped his coffee and arranged his ham sandwich firmly inside his mouth.

Sometimes she went to the post office and bought stamps, and sometimes she went to pick up a card for his wife. Her name was Sonia. He didn't like her very much. That's why he kept buying her flowers; to placate her, to keep her at bay, to stop her from coming into the office. Sonia was bored; they had no children, Sonia was horribly, horribly bored.

They'd tried of course, but something went wrong. It was on his side, weak genes, the little buggers just wouldn't take. His father had had the same problem. Mr Bald was adopted, not many people knew that; only Sonia, and his parents of course. That's what the rows were about, that's why there were flowers, and it was Angela's job to go and fetch them. She tried to vary the arrangements: lilies and pinks with little bursts of gypsum. Roses were too expensive, so sometimes it was a miniature rose, although she thought that looked cheap. Hyacinths some-how didn't. Narcissi were lovely mixed with tulips and catkins.

Once she tried dried flowers, but Mr Bald thought that a foolish idea and asked for his money back. Not an imaginative man, anyone can see that, Angela should have known better. She thought his wife would have liked them. Dried flowers are more practical, they last longer, forever, that's the point. Only any point to flowers if you kept them topped up and fresh.

Dead flowers reek of neglect: curtains left closed, windows unopened, petals fallen to the floor, the sound of crying in the other room. He'd had enough of it. Some things just didn't fit, and you had to accept it. Children weren't for everyone, and his job took up a lot of time. She just needed a hobby. Sonia could be very happy if she tried. Entertain more. They could have the young woman over. I don't expect she has anywhere to go in the evening.

And Mr Bald kept talking, and Ange looked at her bag and thought of Sally and how she loved to swim even in the dead of winter.

A True Anon

'NOT WAVING BUT DROWNING'. They taught us that poem at school. But the man on the shore was waving back. He was a jolly sort. He loved a lark and a jape. He wasn't up for any serious sort of thing, only a fling. All my life I have wondered, who was that man on the shore? An ordinary sort of man strolling along the beach with his stomach sticking out.

There are always people on the beach. People sitting and standing about in clusters: that's why he stood out. Mr Bald, I call him. He was wandering across my line of view. *Wandering* isn't quite the right word. Mr Bald was *sauntering*, and then perhaps *stumbling*, in the way you do when your feet hurt because of pebbles and sand. He was wearing sandals and shorts, perhaps he was wearing a shirt. He was looking for something, for someone. He didn't belong, not to any set, and nobody wants to be in the wrong set when the whistle blows. I have got no further than that. He is a true Anon, a man with a balding head; round, rotund, plump or portly. An avuncular sort, the sort of man pleased to see children out playing nicely together because he has none of his own. Mr Bald has come down to the beach all alone, his wife has gone off on a little holiday. There are such men, a common species, a plain white gull with a protruding beak. All my life I have wanted to ask whether he remembers the child waving back at him. She was a true Anon. But the man on the shore will only scratch his head, and then his belly, and wiggle his toes, and think of the nice young woman in the café along the harbour.

One threadbare Christmas Mum made a whole town from toilet rolls. One Christmas Eve a long time ago, a town magically appeared on the sideboard in our front room; a winter wonderland of open-mouthed choristers. Every knitted head was singing. 'Hark! the Herald Angels' rang through the knitted woods, bouncing off the trees; trees made from toilet rolls covered in deep green wool. Beneath the trees, snow lay thick and crisp and even: layers of cotton wool. A montage of joyful couples stood scattered around, each assigned a snowy glade. Little people dressed in tiny green and red knitted scarves and string gloves. Around their feet – clog-shoes made from corks and buttons tied with tiny bows and laces – lay doll-sized Christmas presents. Each carefully arranged cameo held a snug story, a kind relationship. My mother's imagination was utopian, cheerful and cooperative, communitarian, built around craft and care, hours of invisible work. Nobody in her town was named or known; they were just nice people putting a good face on things. Shopkeepers, clerics, parents and teachers, the lollipop lady, the librarian, the health visitor, the nurse, the man who sweeps the church aisle and buries all the dead, the sexton. My mother taught me to see the people around me: the postman, the newspaper boy, the man at the garage, the mechanic.

Once Mum had had a social life. She lived in a small town, and in the town everyone had jobs and worked. And the town ran, not exactly like clockwork, but it bumped along, and whatever didn't work people tried to fix from their nooks and niches. This is an idealised, old-fashioned view, no doubt, but it would have been Mum's view, and the view of many others. The view that once there had been a sense of daily life, of people passing in the street on the way to run an errand, on the way to work. And on the way you waved: you waved at the people because you knew them. When Mum was growing up people waved a lot because they knew who they were waving at – the town was small enough for that, the people too. And although people left to go elsewhere – the young must leave and grow and have their grand ideas – still there was enough hope that some beauty might arise, and the occasional artist would descend to grace the place.

Mum was an artist; she understood that the world is made better by beauty, and that raising beauty is often an effort. It takes will and imagination, discretion, a carefully managed relationship between inner and outer. She understood that shabbiness can be overcome by a few dignified forms: the neat corners of a pillbox hat, the firm clip of your bag, a piece of well-chosen poetry. Beauty was an occasion requiring accoutrements, and these can bring thunder, lightning and rain, a sudden and surprising change of weather. My mother knew how to smile. Then the sun came out and the bunny rabbits, whose image she drew from her favourite Peter Rabbit books, began to hop, and play. Innocence is a mood and an atmosphere, and my mother carried more than anyone. She understood how to play, to wriggle her nose and twitch her whiskers. Guileless, she knew how to charm.

In another life, my mother would have been adopted by a maiden aunt. Sent to art classes and taught how to dance and sing. Dressed in white satin, she would have been taken out for tea and shown off to other clucking maiden aunts. She would have twitched her nose, taken a bow, and at a graceful moment disappeared off to find her easel. She understood that life can only be survived in partial hiding, by a carefully designed retreat; a fortress of faint lines always partly indecipherable, inscrutable, pressed from white space. I call it poetry.

Margaret Rutherford at the Beach Hotel

IN THE EARLY SUMMER of 1966, the famous English actress Margaret Rutherford went to stay at the Beach Hotel. There was nothing very extraordinary about that, for the Beach Hotel was Margaret's favourite residence outside of London, where flags blew gaily from the windows. Margaret thought this very jolly and pointed it out to her companion, Mr Davis, first name Stringer. It was her habit just as they pulled into the drive to say, 'Look, Stringer, the flags!' And Stringer craned his neck politely to look and see, for this was their habit, before getting out of the car and nodding to the concierge to come and fetch their bags. Those boys were always waiting, and Margaret liked that they came as a pair. Children should come in twos.

Every morning in May and June of 1966, Miss Rutherford was driven from Littlehampton to the Festival Theatre in Chichester for rehearsals of David Garrick's *The Clandestine Marriage*. The hotel was a thirty-minute drive along the coast, passing through the resort of Worthing and another Beach Hotel. I prefer the old-world style of the Littlehampton hotel, she told Mr Stringer, and so they went to Littlehampton. The chairs in the front lounge were terribly comfortable and after morning coffee she sat and wrote her letters and stared through the large bay windows, across the stretch of green, towards the beach. Her view was undisturbed, and so she sat and remembered a whole jumble of things, including Aunt Bessie, whose face kept returning to her just now. Aunt Bessie as Mrs Heidelberg, the lady of the house in Garrick's play.

MRS HEIDELBERG: Do you know that people of quality are expected here this evening? Do be sure that everything is done in the genteelest manner – and to the honour of the family.

MRS HEIDELBERG: Get the dining-room in order as soon as possible. Unpaper the curtains, take the covers off the couch and the chairs, and put the china figures on the mantle-piece immediately.

MRS HEIDELBERG: I declare there is not such a thing to be seen now, as a young woman with a fine waist – You all make yourselves as round as Mrs Deputy Barter.

MRS HEIDELBERG: Lord! D'ye think a man of fashion, as he is, can't distinguish between the genteel and the vulgar part of the family? Between you and your sister, for instance – or me and my brother? Be advised by me, child! It is all politeness and good-breeding. Nobody knows the quality better than I do.

MRS HEIDELBERG: Pray now, brother, mind how you behave. I am always in a fright about you with people of quality.

Now the rehearsals were over, Margaret could settle into a new routine. The car came to pick her up for the evening show at five o'clock. She waited in the front lounge for Stringer to go back up to his room to check that nothing had been forgotten. This was his way, he was a punctilious sort, and Margaret was too: there was an hour for tea, never less, never more, and always Earl Grey. She took her tea to the theatre; they know how she likes it there. Ever so hot, just off the boil, not too much milk. China nice and thin. She drinks the first cup straight down like a shot.

But we're rushing, and Margaret wouldn't like that. Let's go back to the car journey, that leisurely spin along the coast from Littlehampton to Chichester one fine day in June 1966. You can take the A259 all the way. I wonder if, when driving, or being driven I should say – Margaret was chauffeured – she hummed that tune she became so famous for: that jaunty little tune that started up the Miss Marple films. Rapid fiddling and baroque finger work on the harpsichord; it skips along very quickly, wheels turning ever so fast, you can barely keep up: that lovely old Daimler, there it goes, *do you see it?*

Deep blue, to match the sea, Miss Rutherford is spinning along. Now she winds down the window and puts her face out to smell the salt air. She sniffs exaggeratedly, but that's just her face, you might say. It's floppy and saggy; one critic said she looked like a lovable pet cow. There is something cow-like about her face, and cows are affable creatures, gentle and sympathetic.

Miss Rutherford is spinning along; it's a good thirty or forty minutes to the theatre. Mr Davis is sitting quietly next to her with his eyes closed. Sometimes he gets motion sickness, so Margaret opens the window. As they come into Worthing, she leans a little further out to look at the Marine Hotel.

'A rather ugly building really, far too modern. What year do you think it was built, Stringer? Nineteen-twenty, nineteen-twenty-two . . . and full of flappers!'

Mr Stringer doesn't answer. He's Mr Stringer in the films, always there by her side; Stringer Davis, her live-in husband, home help, domestic, her companion, but right now, poor Mr Stringer is feeling rather queasy.

'Shall we stop the car, dear? You do look ever so queer.'

'No, I'm fine. Let's keep moving along, Margaret. I don't want us to be late. You know you hate being late.'

Miss Rutherford leans forward and taps the shoulder of the driver who looks back at her through the rearview mirror. 'Another twenty minutes, Samuel, is that right?'

'That's right, Mrs Rutherford. Another twenty minutes or so, the roads are clear.'

'Miss Rutherford, Sam.'

Which wasn't strictly speaking true, but actresses like to keep up appearances.

'What a pretty girl . . . Stringer, look? Can you see her? What a lovely head of hair, lovely posture too. I expect she's had some training; she'd make a lovely actress. Stringer, can you see her . . . are you looking . . . Stringer! She's wearing a bow in her hair, or is it a scarf? Oh dear, you do look rather peaky. Open your window, dear, open it up, come on, let's get some air in here, some lovely fresh air.'

And Margaret leaned over and wound down the window.

'Oh dear, am I squashing you?'

'No, dear, it's fine. I think I shall close my eyes for a minute.'

'I am sorry you missed that girl. She was simply splendid. I wonder if she works in the hotel?'

And so they proceeded, along the seafront and out the other side of town, with Margaret chatting and rehearsing some of her more awkward lines; and by the time they pulled into Chichester, Stringer, known as Mr Davis to most, was snoring, and Margaret had to gently nudge him awake.

Aunt Clara

MARGARET RUTHERFORD never had children. Some people can't, and some people don't, because they are themselves still children. Margaret was one of those, and she loved children as a way of loving herself. There she is, in the film *Sister Clara*, playing the kindly maiden aunt who loves to tell stories about bunnies and badgers frolicking in the summer sun.

Meanwhile, the adults in the room are concerned with adult business; they are reading the family will. And Clara's face is smirking and puckering up like a rabbit as she tries to catch the children's attention. Margaret has one of those faces: now she is a bunny, now she is a hare, running across the field towards the badger.

Later, on another day, after she has inherited all the money from the estate of her late uncle Simon, who liked Clara better than anyone in his family, Clara goes to the races. She goes to the races with Henry, her late uncle's butler, who is a gobby sort; and at the races Henry the butler watches the horses racing along, while Clara sees only rabbits.

'So, the pretty animal rabbit put on his purple muffler and set off to find the place where the badger brothers lived, but he hadn't got that far before.'

'Clara!'

'When who do you think he saw bounding over the ditch.'

'Clara! Clara, be quiet!'

'Oh, oh, I am so sorry, I do apologise. Shh, children, shh, we must be terribly quiet.'

'But it was all all right in the end and they all had a wonderful picnic.'

The children smile and the will is read.

'To my niece Clara Hilton!'

Clara gets all the money, innocence wins out, and the rabbit hops across the field and takes her place in paradise. However, before she leaves this earth, Clara settles her late uncle's estate and arranges money to be left to poor little mites who can't afford to go on holiday. 'My children's holiday fund,' she says, over and over to the fancy people who come to hear her music concert. But the fancy people do not listen, they are too busy sipping their tea.

Maiden aunts get bees in their bonnets about children going to the seaside. Children must play and build sandcastles; wet their feet in the sea; feel the salt in their hair; climb the breakwaters; roam through the dunes and cliffs; ride a donkey and eat an ice cream every other day. Clara is a romantic, Clara is a child, Clara must wet her feet on Worthing sands.

'To my niece Clara Hilton, the only one of you who won't drink away the profits.'

So Clara inherits a pub; she inherits a racecourse; she inherits a house for women who offer their services to men. And the woman known as Aunt Clara, exclaims, '*But why me?*'

*

When she speaks her chin waggles, and her mouth rumples up into dough. Margaret Rutherford has a doughy face and big doughy rims beneath her cow-like eyes. She has a kind face, but Margaret was also a sad woman, perhaps because she didn't have children of her own, that's the obvious case. Instead, she adopted waifs and strays, and I suspect Mr Stringer was a calf to her cow, but it was all right in the end because they had a wonderful picnic in a village called Chalfont St Peter. And Margaret spent time in her beloved garden, and time in the village wiping local brows. She was that sort of woman, ever so kind. Think of Aunt Clara and her love of children and those who remain: those four girls in that house on Lipton Grove run by Mrs Gladys Smith where dear Uncle Simon used to go. 'Gladys, one of the only creatures for whom I had true affection,' said Uncle Simon and Aunt Clara heard that and thought, My, who would have thought it? Uncle Simon in love with a house of fallen women: Gladys and Edna, Edith and Elsie and Phyllis and Dolly – and Clara looked carefully at the woman who'd just entered the room to say 'cheerio' and couldn't help herself from saying, 'Dolly's not at all young, is she?'

'No,' said Gladys, who went by Mrs Smith. At her age it was hardly likely she was anything else. 'We're none of us young.'

'Cheerio, Glady, dear, lovely weather for it, I don't think!'

And Aunt Clara watches the woman cross the room and go out through the other side, as though she's on stage. But the audience is waning, she can't keep the punters; still a few tag along, and there she goes, through one door and out the other, all tarted up and ready for business. Dolly with her pink lipstick on. Coral, she says to Gladys as she passes through.

'How does it look, Glad?'

'Precious. You look precious, Dolly.' And Dolly closes the door.

Gladys is a sensitive soul. She has intuition, that deep spring that never dries up no matter what you do. Gladys guesses Aunt Clara is ill. It's in her eyes.

'How did you know?'

Gladys is kind, Gladys has always been kind, and Clara nods. 'So things must be settled.'

She hears Uncle Simon's voice:

UNCLE SIMON: I am leaving this all to my niece Clara
    because she was the only one too busy looking after other
    people to come to my party and so I know I can entrust
    her to look after the welfare of the only living creatures for
    whom I have real affection, Julie Mason, Henry Martin,
    my six greyhounds, and Mrs Gladys Smith.
CLARA: Dear Uncle Simon, I will do my best.

And she does. She moves into Uncle Simon's house and takes up with Henry, the domestic.

'Henry, it would make me very happy if you'd stay and carry on exactly as before.'

HENRY: Exactly?
AUNT CLARA: Exactly.
HENRY: It wouldn't work. The neighbours would start
    talking.
AUNT CLARA: About what?

HENRY: About you and me. You see, you're a spinster and I
am too. And you're a woman, I mean a lady, and I'm a man.
AUNT CLARA: Let them talk, Henry. The talk will do them
good! I need a helping hand.

The Child Eccentric

MARGARET RUTHERFORD was a household name in my family home, often evoked when someone was pulling a face. Margaret wore herself on her face, which made her a good actress, but it also made her a cross child; for such a person can wear appalling expressions and go further with her face than any of us.

Margaret played the determined, amiable child, out and about with her handbag; out and about clearing up crimes and disorder. Her face was a thick daub sponge for all sorts of petty misrule. That was her role in *Aunt Clara*, the kind relative who came to sort things out. That was also her Miss Marple, who made her famous, a character with gumption and nerve.

Everyone listens to Miss Marple because Miss Marple always knows; she intuits. And what is intuition but an underground spring? Something stored away in deep reserves bringing back rich salt and minerals. Scatter it carefully, it is rare; and it isn't something you can learn, but something you are born with, quite innate, and eccentricity is its soulmate: the settled state of the child who intuits what proud adults will not know is there. Some are fortunate enough to hold onto it if nobody peels it away.

Margaret Rutherford was the child who intuits the situation before the situation has even begun. As a young girl she was sent to live with her Aunt Bessie in Wimbledon. Bessie was another eccentric sort whose house was already quite full of people. Three floors, and plenty of room for Margaret to roam about practising.

So Margaret was encouraged to go out into the garden – you'll have more space, more fun, and Margaret dear, you can practise your faces there – and so Aunt Bessie, *dear Aunt Bessie*, whose last name was Nicholson, encouraged her young ward to start *acting*. And so, there she was, young Margaret in 1895, feeling – as she said herself – like a bantam hen with her auburn-coloured hair and her round penny-green eyes. Eyes dropped into a pool and turned a little rusty perhaps; eyes playing dress up and make believe in a leafy garden near Wimbledon High Street and Wimbledon Park, not far from the girls' school, where she was known as *Peggy Who Could Act*. Her first part was Jack from a set of nursery rhymes set to songs called quadrilles.

And Peggy stood and sang and danced in the way she was instructed, overseen by neat and clean Miss Hastings. And Jack played opposite Jill, a girl called Bridget, but poor Jill – Margaret with her pouty crumpled face fiercely twitching, reversed the role you might expect Jack to play, and pushed Jill down the hill and stole the show. For she had that gift we call comedy which can turn everything on its head; and suddenly Miss Hastings and Miss Braithwaite and Miss Juniper are holding their sides and laughing: because by then her funny face was working and bringing the house down. 'In the garden, Margaret, please.'

'In the garden,' they called, and Margaret's nose wrinkled and twitched. Her face was working.

Until there was a knock at the door and a dirty and dishevelled person appeared on the step and told Margaret that her father was a murderer and that he had been locked away in a place called Broadmoor. And Margaret swivelled and squirmed on the doorstep and her face changed colour. It is a terrible thing to be told your father has killed another man. Is the caller a tramp? Is this her father or a criminal like him? Her mind begins to race; she is shaking. She will go and find Aunt Bessie and tell her about the Man at the Door.

The story is a muddled one, but Aunt Bessie made it clear that *everything had been a terrible accident,* and that poor William, her father, was not in his right mind when he took an axe – or was it a knife – to his own father. Aunt Bessie was sure to omit the details for they were too sordid, but only to say that William Rutherford Benn was not in his right mind.

'He always had a taste for the theatre, poor William, and no doubt it was a row that went too far. He never meant to hurt his father, they were terribly close, and you know, Margaret dear, we all have to work on our tempers, but your father was not in his right mind when he lifted – well – *when it happened*. William was a kindly soul, gentle and learned; he loved nothing more than poetry and music, like you, dear. But he'd been terribly worn down and his father had taken him off to the country for a bit of a rest – Julius was a lovely man who loved his son –oh dear.'

Aunt Bessie began to blink; the child was shaking, her chin was wobbling, lifting.

'He was a gentle man, dear, very kind, your father was a very kind man. You must remember that. He loved poetry and music and used to compose lovely little songs, do you remember any, dear?'

The child was staring at the ground.

'No, no, how foolish of me. Now let's go and see what we can have for tea. I think it might be time to get Amy to go and get some cake. What sort of cake would you like, Margaret dear? A nice fruit cake . . . a currant cake?'

Gladys Smith

Such is the tone of maiden aunts as they console orphaned children. And Mrs Gladys Smith in the house on Lipton Grove in Paddington, *how do we console you?* Gladys who I recognise from other places; Gladys who reminds me of my aunt: her way of drawing her breath so until she almost stops breathing, her bleak look. Her staring through the grey nylon curtains sullied with all that smoke. Her grey veil. My Aunt Di in the front room of our terraced house looking bleakly into the future – another lost soul. She reminds me of Gladys. Gladys who *does* look bleak. But Gladys, there have always been girls like you, *and whose child are you?*

Not a girl anymore, am I? Gladys knows that for her it is too late. She can't be saved by some maiden aunt. *This is me lot, and I'll take it.* Lost souls wander, and to anyone on the outside, one Gladys is very much like another. A cruel thought, she thinks, but underneath her puckered skin, Gladys is still a child.

Gladys, are you listening? No. She is staring out through the plane trees, cigarette dangling from her mouth. Gladys is fond of her fags; they sit nicely between her teeth. *Stop me eating, don't they?* So her waist is nice and slim. We all need a bit of help with our figure, and Gladys is getting on. The gin helps, and she goes towards the drinks cabinet as the old lady gabbles on.

'Isn't there something else they could do? Laundry work?'

Gladys laughs. She laughs and laughs, that high-pitched, queer laugh. Laundry work! Somehow it always comes back to laundry, dirty old sheets ragged and torn and no place to wash them. 'Hang them out between the trees,' her mother used to say, where the bark is rough. 'That'll 'old 'em nice and firm.' Sheets ragged and torn and darned around the edges. Not fit to be seen in public. 'Cover 'em up – there – between the trees, you fool!'

One washday the wind got up and whipped them right away. Gladys saw them fly across the yard. She watched, mesmerised, as the big white kites took off, up over the old fence. Flapping and flapping until the trees got them and they were strangled.

'I tol' yer to tie them tight wi' pegs.'

'But we don' 'ave no pegs. They're all gone.'

'Git outta here! Git outta my sight.'

Gladys sucked from her glass. They had no ice; the freezer was broken. She remembered they'd had to forfeit their supper for a few days to afford new sheets. Then suddenly sheets appeared. Her mother had had a word, or someone had had a word, and some do-gooding spinster in the village had dragged them out from her linen chest. Gladys could still recall the smell – musty and furry – straight from a cat basket, she reckoned.

Old spinsters slept with their cats. She looked at the old woman in front of her with her puffy face. Rising dough, Gladys thought, nice and puffy and ready to go into the oven. She was smiling at her, head cocked sideways, awaiting her response. *What makes such a woman solicitous of a woman like me?*

She feels sorry for you, Gladys, can't you see? Sorry for your common manners and your cheap way of talking. You help yourself to a drink, but you don't ask the old girl. I suppose you assume spinsters don't touch drink. Still, you should ask. The old woman was making her nervous. Talk of money always made her nervous. What did she want?

'Uncle Simon wanted to make sure you were provided for; he was especially fond of you, Gladys.' Yes, thought Gladys, in his own way perhaps he was, silly old bugger.

'I don't mean to interfere . . . but you can't go on like this, my dear.' The old lady's face was beginning to pucker and tear.

'You see, Gladys, I've known girls like you . . .'

'*Girl?* Well thank you very much!' And Gladys grins. 'He used ter call me that too. So what yer want ter tell me? To pack it all in?'

Men come and go in 1 Lipton Grove, and the beds creak. Gladys only does one once a week. On Thursdays, after lunch, a bit of ham and cheese, she trots off in her patent black heels to the man with the mountainous belly. She can't see his face over it. He huffs and he puffs, and he blows his house down. Never lasts more than five minutes. A storm in a teacup. Gladys smokes her fag across the mountain and thinks of that time she was in Switzerland as an au pair. The air was so clean and fresh.

'Open the window, love.' The mountain shakes and turns over.

She pulls up the sash and the curtains rip. Cheap nylon. Tut-tut. Gladys shakes her head and turns back to the room.

'So will that do you?'

'Lovely, pet, just fine. 'Ere, come and sit by me.' And he pets the bed and the warm sheets where she was flat on her back a minute ago.

'Would yer like to go away wiv me, Gladys, to the seaside?'

'I can't afford the time orf, Pete. You know I can't. I've got a business to run.'

'I'll pay yer rent, Gladys. Forget about that. We'd have a luverly time.'

'I don't mix business and pleasure, Pete.'

'Oh drop the form'lities, Glad. We know one anuver too well.'

'Do we now? I don't know as you know me, Pete. What's me fav'rite colour?'

'Red.'

'No it ain't, it's yeller, the colour of the sun.'

'A real romantic, ain't we?'

'Beneath all this cheap tat I'm quite a classy lady.'

'Oh I know tha' pet. I've seen yer in bed, remember.'

'You don't know th' first thing about me. What I show yer in bed ain't anything to do wi' me. Tha's the first rule of play. Don't yer know that? Anyhow, I've got business to attend to. Said I'd go and see th' old lady.'

'What old lady?'

'The one who came th' other day. She's got something important ter tell me, about her dying.'

'What her dying go' to do with you?'

'She knows I know.'

'What are you on about? Who is this old bird anyway?'

'That's what I'm gonna find out. So you'll have ter hold yer horses wi' yer seaside outing.'

Edna May

SHE ONLY WENT TO evening prayers because she never fancied the morning service. That was his service: for meeting and greeting and nodding his head the way they do when men talk business without talking. Never staying too long, just long enough that people knew you were there. So they knew he was a busy man. While she stayed at home and pared the vegetables and put out the washing. While she listened to the wireless playing through the kitchen window. Packed up the remaining pegs and went back inside. Put on a pan of milk mixed with water for her coffee and watched it froth while the service played on around her. From Ely this week, very grand. E-lie, E-ly, a strange sort of name: ancient, forgotten, sitting among flat fields near Cambridge? Where did it all go, the names, the places; everything had run away from her.

He who would valiant be, 'gainst all disaster.

The voices soared above the organ, and she could see the pipes with their fat notes billowing out down the aisles. Notes feeding the mouths of the congregation as they made shapes, some mute, some heard. Church was a place for bellowing. Against those pipes you can do an awful lot. Scream your lungs out if you follow the tune. You can practically go deaf when the pipes start to blow and fume.

Di-sars-ter. The organ trembled and her thick rich notes went underground. Someone was being buried. You had to stand up to it: disaster, misfortune, a run of bad luck. You couldn't let life trample over you like that. Edna looked up. Her sister Gladys on the beach, hair all torn and whipped around her face. *Gladys, Gladys, where are you?* But Gladys was too far out all her life and now it was too late. Dear Gladys with the sheepish face rising up from the ground grinning. Gladys was always grinning, even when she was drowning.

Is that what happened?

Is it?

Is that what you say?

What you told Mother?

Edna wasn't very musical, but she remembered the crashing sound of the waves. *Gladys, Gladys, come back!*

Fred had the music, but she knew what she liked: old hymns and waltzes, the foxtrot, the Charleston. Never been sure about the jive: too vigorous, too sexual, too American. Gladys had liked to jive, and Edna tipped back her head and closed her eyes and thought back to her dancing days.

On the edge of the shore with the gulls, with a boy, with her sister sitting on the pebbles fiddling with her skirt.

'Edie, Edie, come on!'

For Gladys it was always time to go, the girl is never calm, her mother said. Gladys on the pebbles, folding and unfolding her petticoat, holding onto her hat, feebly calling through the wind – Gladys the baby. Gladys with her toothy grin.

'What's wrong with her?' asked Cyril. 'Can't you send her away?'

'She's just being a ninny. Ignore her, come on. Four and four, Cyril, then four and six. Count to four then add two. One-two-three-four, then five-six, slower. That's the foxtrot. You have to follow the music. Can you hear it? Watch, look, watch my feet!'

'You look like a penguin, Edie, that's not right. Let me show you.'

And the tall man pulls the slight girl to him and puts his arm around her shoulder; they dip down together towards the sand. She falls backwards, then forwards, following the line of his arm, dipping and dipping, down.

'It's like water, Edie. Imagine a long wave of water, flowing over you. Water, Edie, water, turn yourself into water!'

Water and wine, the body of Christ, the hymn was still playing but it was a different one. *All Things Bright and Beautiful.* She could hear children's voices, sweet and sincere, little faces lined up. Points of light travelling from the stained-glass windows dropping down upon their cheeks and noses. Little birds, she said, half out loud, robins and blue tits, they must be *hungry. Feed the birds.* Gladys had always liked to put out bread for the birds, even on windy days. She never noticed what happened to the crumbs – but Edna did – she just didn't tell Gladys, because Gladys would never listen.

Mary Sleeps

WE SLEEP AND we don't know where we go, only that we shuttle back and forth across a dark line. Mary went with her smile, and it was as bright as the star of Bethlehem. No one was with her, not even Miss Travis, who was due the following morning with her shopping. Mary was reading her Blake when she quietly slipped away to join the bright beauty of the stars.

To anyone on the outside, Miss Mary Neal, born Clara Sophia, was simply dozing in her chair. Soon, she would stir to get her supper. The orange lamp was on, and the curtains were open. Seven o'clock in the evening on St Flora's Road, Littlehampton and soft summer light filtering through the curtains. She can hear the birds singing on the other side of the window. Shadows flickering in and out between the lace. Midsummer. A warm evening. Plenty of time before bed. Mary feels soft and drowsy.

There is a book open on her lap – William Blake – she's always liked his simple rhymes. Knows them off by heart.

I wander thro' each charter'd street,
Near where the charter'd Thames does flow.
And mark in every face I meet
Marks of weakness, marks of woe.

Mary was dreaming of her London days. All those poor faces. Had they really helped them, those little sods, with not enough to feed or clothe themselves?

In every cry of every Man,
In every Infant's cry of fear,
In every voice: in every ban,
The mind-forg'd manacles I hear.

I would ban any sort of man who made a child work like that. Mary nods.

How the chimney-sweepers cry
Every blackning Church appalls,
And the hapless Soldiers sigh
Runs in blood down Palace walls.

I would ban any sort of man who made a child cry like that. She sees his face, the little chimney sweep in the cellar. 'I ain't eat nuffin' since yesterday.' The sweet rich smell of pastry, his mouth covered in crumbs, his black fingernails. 'Can I 'ave some more?'

Mary nods again. London is full of jewels and riches shining in the noonday sun. Just don't look too far behind St Pancras, or any railway station where the chimney sweepers cry for their mams laid out to rest in the front room, surrounded by blackening faces. Heads of hapless woe. Mary's head falls forward. Now she is thinking of her girls. How they jumped and sang, even on rooftops. Her flat in Somerset Terrace, six floors up, she shared with Emmeline. On warm summer evenings they came up to practise their dancing. What a sight that must have been! Girls in white bonnets springing up and down on the skyline. A set of cotton frocks skipping behind the railings. White fluffy ducks bobbing through the clouds. And in the corner, a fiddler waggling his bow back and forth, tipping and turning to catch the dip of his bow, the tune, the tread of those girls on the rooftop, clippety-clop. Mary smiles and turns her head. And now the image moves, as images do, down towards the street. A young boy delivering the evening news turns the corner and stops to stare. Giant white flowers, white balloons, sacks of flowers, enormous ghosts, puppets, what are those? He hears the music rise and swell and cranes his neck further. Girls – he can hear their shrieks – girls. How did they get there? Where is the ladder, where are the steps?

The child on the street below swivels his head and turns to look up at the clouds. They are moving faster now, and the wind is lifting. A spit of rain on his cheek. Slashes of wet. They'll have to come down soon. A shriek, a large shriek startles him and he turns himself the right way round. One of the white flowers has sunk to the ground. A white stamen dangling over, a leg, a head.

Six floors down and the shrieks are loud enough to draw people out. White flowers gather round on the rooftop and a body flops slightly towards the terrace edge. Something flaps and falls, a pink ribbon. The boy holds his breath. Mary holds hers. The child rises from the ground and pulls the ribbon behind her. She is smiling. The ribbon floats through the air, and the child lifts her legs and begins to resume those old steps she knows so well. Clippety-clop.

And Mary sleeps, hearing the echo of London in her ears, when through midnight streets she used to wander with her friend Emmeline, often quite ungodly hours, when they could not sleep, discussing the nature of their club for girls and the riots they had seen. *Girls from such poor homes are often riotous; it is difficult to bring form to those who have had no love or discipline.* They keep the unruliest of hours, 'not to be abed after midnight is to be up betimes', so says Sir Toby Belch, though that is the wrong sort of Shakespeare for my girls. They are out in the cold like Poor Tom, and who *gives anything to poor Tom? Away! The foul fiend follows me! Through the sharp hawthorn blows the cold wind. Hum! go to thy cold bed and warm thee. Emmeline, let us go in for tea!*

Her Name was Verity

I WANT TO write of 'We'. 'We' is all the people left behind once you start looking. There are bodies everywhere, like fallen trees. Some I know and some I do not know. 'We' includes everyone I can think of the morning of 16 October 1987: all those stranded looking from windows the morning after the Great Storm. Mary Neal was dead by then, long gone. Mary died 22 June 1944, the day the Russians were finishing off the German Panzers, sixteen days after the Allies launched themselves across the beaches of Normandy. Mary left just when the war was being won; as American troops were entering Cherbourg; as they were crossing the harbour, as they were climbing the wall.

On 19 June 1944, a storm broke out that lasted for four days. The Allies were hurled against the harbour wall, their anchors scraping, scraping desperately to find a hold. One poor man sent by the *Daily Mail* saw it all. Binks was his name. Poor Binks, clinging to whatever bit of land he could find, any holding hand.

And the water flew over the side of the boat, a raging white monster, lashing her tongue over the sodden men. Binks held on. He lay low to the bottom of the craft and didn't murmur a word except his prayers, silently clasped between his teeth.

Binks was a Catholic boy; he shut his eyes and looked for Mary, but Mary was rolling through the boiling foam. *Mary, Mother of God, blessed art thee among women, and blessed is the fruit of thy womb. Save us sinners from a wretched death. Keep us safe this night. Thomas Binks, a True Anon, who will write up your tale?*

And the boat ripped through the teeth of the gale; and the patrol boat, which had once seemed so sturdy, was reduced to a miserable wretch. But the captain clung on – Parsons was his name – a decent chap from a small town in Hampshire called Whitchurch; and Parsons turned the helm hard towards the waves and the boat drove her course through the furious white lips of the monster.

That night Binks began to believe in sea monsters, for he saw them with his own eyes, that white Knucker that surged towards them, making more and more babies from the waves. She was foaming at the mouth, and she was bitter, for she had expected her mate to come that evening from the tropics; but instead he came from the Atlantic with his sharp jaws and took a bite out of many a berth.

A furious monster is a hungry monster, flaring up from the eight-foot waves, growing to twenty by the middle of the night. Binks watched helplessly as the waves consumed other craft; as they darted in and out of her teeth, looking for shelter. In the leeward side of a fleet of ships tucked far from the grey Normandy beach on 19 June, two days before midsummer.

No one slept that night, they only clung to whatever they could, praying for the wind to abate, the waves to calm, for the Knucker to go down to the sandy bottom. Fury drove her on, blind fury, this angry sea-dragon, who writhed and lashed her way across the concrete floor. And Binks began to wonder where the legs of the *caisson* started and how far down she goes. Phoenix, they called her, a harbour made from floating concrete, six islands for towing in the Allies, *what a master plan!*

But Binks must stick to the facts. He must close in on factual evidence. No flab, no fear or terror, no raging atmosphere. No poetry. They are somewhere in the English Channel, but where exactly, and how far from shore? *Somewhere beneath lay an indecipherable mass of concrete, Mulberry A, a metal harbour blown to pieces on north-easterly winds.*

He must report.

I must report.

And Binks, lying

on the radio room floor,

pressed his ear seaward.

A crash and something heavy hits the floor – the typewriter, its metal carriage shuttling like a small cannon, clips his ear.

Somewhere an indecipherable mass of concrete hit my head and the metal harbour was blown sideways towards the shore.

And I, Tom Binks, christened Thomas, after the apostle, cannot feel my legs. Where are my hands, where is my head, I cannot feel my feet?

But this cannot go into his report. There must be no confession. Leave that to the priest who can see everything if he wishes through his narrow grille, can hear your breathing – the heavy weight of his lungs collapsing seaward – oh Binks – something is covering your mouth!

Azure blue, topaz blue, the blue of forget-me-nots –
it is important to get it right, the colour of the sea.
    blue forget-me-nots.
And now, this is the end, thinks Binks.
Thomas Binks, a True Anon,
shall die at sea
    with men and monsters he does not know.

Miss Cull says she knows. She told the policeman she knew. *I know*, she said, *I know what I saw.* In the end, all we can know is what we see: so many things falling from the sky, the night of the Great Storm. That night I dreamed a child died, but it was an old dream, and an old name, and her name was Gladys and she left me with murderous feelings.

Ghosts leave feelings. My mother, my grandmother and the woman on the train. *Not a scarf, not a hat, but a pearl necklace, that is the important fact.* Someone pulled it hard from her: that pair of hands closing in around her puckered neck. *Time to go*, they said, but who decides that?

Iris Henderson knows exactly when it was the old lady went. *When was the last time you saw her?* they ask. But they do not listen for the answer, for they do not wish to know. *In the carriage opposite me, just before I fell asleep, the old lady was there.* She was there, and she was smiling, and she had begun to sing her song, the one about the white cliffs of Dover.

It is the same old dream. The train is clickety-clacking along, and on the train, everyone is singing. They are singing songs of Valentines, of love and marriage and happy ever after. There are happy endings, and the ending has already begun because the people are leaving the holiday behind. *Holidays can be so difficult. So unpredictable, the weather, the accommodation, the mattresses, the crossing, the route taken, the train, oh the train! So unpredictable!* The whole train joins in and the people make a chorus, an ode to joy, because they are returning, because they had been stuck for a while; but now they are moving again, and the train is passing through a tunnel, a deep burrow through the Alps. *Are we on the German or the Swiss side? Are we in France?* The people do not know, but they are red-cheeked and singing as though they were outside, running and chafing against the wind. As though the whole of the white world of snowy mountains and green-peaked tips were thawing. It is spring and the snow is beginning to melt; there is some mercy, there is hope. And the edelweiss flower in the shape of a studded star is showing herself as a ring, a white engagement ring. And the people peek out from the carriage – these two carriages, this one and the dining car – and they being to sing their happy song. Voices pushing up against the oak-lined ceiling of the car, a song of returning from afar. To that pretty seaside town where the price of mackerel is cheaper than anywhere and the salt clings to your nails. *You will have to soak your fingers to get it off!* That bright white jewel on your index finger. *Digitus secundus.* That little gem you bought in the market. *The price was terribly good.* You set your heart on her, a pearl in the shape of a flower, and so the people sing.

'Write down the contents of your dream,' Mum said. 'All artists must dream.' And Miss Cull says, for she writes down anything strange in her journal, that the night of the storm she saw a boy below her building – *a very tall block of flats, twelve floors up, Inspector, and I was looking down, and he was looking up, and our eyes met.* A small boy wearing a cap and craning his neck. Craning, she says, because he resembled a bird looking up at the sky. And that's when the flower fell. *Paper whites, paper whites, paper whites, see how they smell? Who said that?* Miss Cull continues. *The body hit the ground hard, I heard it, Inspector, all the way up here.* And when he heard that, the policeman lowered his head. Miss Cull swears it was a girl. Lost souls wander. Miss Cull knows this.

'Better to cover them up, Inspector.'

'Cover what up, ma'am?'

'The dead and gone, the poppets, those underneath the soil. Cover them with flowers, their souls are bare.'

The policeman doesn't know, and I don't know, but Miss Cull says she saw a falling flower. 'For the truth will betray us all in the end, Inspector. Her name was Verity.'

'Are you sure you weren't dreaming, ma'am? Closed your eyes for a moment; it happens to us all?' The lady in front of him looks old and tired. Her face is pale and crinkly. Her hair flecked with white.

'Write down the contents of your dream,' Mum said. 'Your dreams will tell you what you do not know.'

'I know what I saw, Inspector. I saw a girl falling. Fair hair, blue eyes, a real poppet of a thing. A white flower falling, a paper bird. None of us looks quite the same in flight.'

JOSEPH MALLORD WILLIAM TURNER would be happy to spy girls such as Gladys and Hilda perched on the cliff. They offer some relief: a shape, an outline. Two local women watching the men on the beach beneath; fishermen unknotting their nets. The light dipping into the water. Few people, little history, only the outlines of the harbour basin and the church spire reaching for the sky. Only the orchestra of light moving slowly; the movements of his hands scraping back the paper. Transparent, translucent, white shallows turning deeper, tinged with gold.

Gladys and Hilda are there but their heads are bent, bonnets turned downwards: voices lost on the wind, on the flap of ribbon and string. Local women sharing tales and taunts of local lads and lasses. Young women there to watch their men. Gossip and engagements. Broken hearts mended. Men lost and found at sea. Feet hardened by salt water, split open by pebbles. If I could get close to their hands, I would see that they are rough and callused. Hard hills of skin stitching together ripped nets, torn calico sacks. I must fill in the details because the writer cannot leave things alone. She must agitate, trace, draw out the words. Listen to the people speak.

But the women's faces are turned against us. We cannot see their smiles and smirks, their dimpled chins, their moving lips, their words. We cannot see their hands. Busy hands bobbing up and down as they lay out the sheets, repair flour sacks, bind up broken nets. Old hands, worn hearts and minds, familiar chatter as they watch the men hauling up their boats. Fishermen returning from a catch. White bonnets bobbing, birds. White bonnets, sails. White bonnets, calico bags, this is how the painter sees them. And the men long and lean as wooden planks, climbing from narrow boats onto a bullock's cart that will carry them from shore to town. Now, this is the writer seeing. The painter sees the outline of the form, and only he knows what lies within. We cannot hear their chatter and smirks. The wind sucks out all the noise.

Last night was a rough crossing, today there is calm, the waves are low and gentle. Local men going about their business, tidying up the shore. The writer sees human commerce: hands waving, girlish flirtation, a handkerchief raised in hope of being noticed. But for the painter they are nothing more than raw material; white shapes rising, plump body life. It is the writer who wants to be noticed; it is her hand raised, waving vigorously, anxiously, hoping to be spotted, seen. She is waving to her grandmother, her grandmother's relatives, the ghosts of her ancestors. She is waving to Mary. Mary made from scraps and shards, pearls, fragments of bone. Mary made from gathered shells. The writer is a shell seeker; she must unturn, uncover, she cannot leave them alone, those old worn pearls. She wants them shiny: she adds threads, connections, buttons and fastenings, hooks, and eyes, stays. They must stay for her, these women, and the writer holds her breath. Will they leave; will they vanish? How can she fasten them down? She must make a brooch, a cameo, she must draw the outline of their face. But she cannot draw, and so she must pillage for leftovers and scraps. Steal buttons. Take cuttings. Snip off a badge. Lay out her shells upon the windowsill as her grandmother did. Pay homage to her past. Inherit.

While the painter sees only pools of colour and light, raggedy forms, oblivion. He is not afraid of not seeing. He is not afraid of the dark or the light. For now he sketches; later he will paint. Water running across the canvas this way and that; pools of water streaking across the white, stopping and starting, melting and eddying. He adds more paint, more gum to fasten it to his paper. Now he smells honey. Paint is a sharp and sweet thing, distracting. He licks his fingers; tiny mounds stuck to the surface of papery threads. He mixes the small cake-paint with water and presses down hard. She dissolves, no settling, no relaxing. Above all, the swift smooth flight of the arm, the fingers, the hand. Moving fast across the paper, dipping in and out of the paint. Memory must be remade before he loses it, that wheeling motion, the flight of the bird.

An artist never quite tells the story in front of him. He alters, remakes, repairs. Omits, removes, blanks out, washes away the remnants. The artist wants to start again, to make the world over; it is his vision, his confidence, his way of seeing things. The artist and the writer are relatives, but she must depend upon the remnants. Clutch at what is there. Wire basket, calico sheets, torn stays, shredded netting: she wants to touch and finger these, to feel their nerves. Worn hands and shredded knuckles, torn ligaments from missed steps as they trip down the chalky cliff, as they look out to sea – to the men – to the beach, the horizon, the choppy future. Broken ankles, the jutting bones, she runs her hands over their worn soles. Unties the laces, picks out the pebbles, scrapes back the leather.

Joseph Mallord William Turner wants the light. He does not care whether the women on the cliff are washerwomen or oyster catchers, laundry women or sewing girls; whether they pick mussels as they chat or pull seaweed from the basket next to them.

In his damp studio in Chelsea, the painter's hand moves over them; caresses their cheeks and sees their claws moving; their white flapping bonnets; their small, dimpled sails. *Small crabs*, he mutters, *scuttle away*. What matters is the sky, the water, the crescent of the sun, her basking glory. But still I agitate, I must know: who are the women with white flapping ears; bonnets falling over their faces? I cannot leave them. So I poke and prod, because the writer must have her biography; she must supervise lives: instruct, give orders, arrange time and space, thread and rethread, tread back and forth over their lives. Her eyes hurt from all that looking; her mouth sore from all her questioning. It is her need, it is her want, her will and way to make things move when all is still except the waves. The writer is never still; her hands fly, her neck swivels and turns, her eyes on the ground and in the air. She treads.

Her boots are worn from moving them about, the women, the people. She has been down to the shore so often she smells the salt air in her dreams. She converses with the salt, the hunched women, and the women talk back. Their mouths begin to move; they chatter, they work, they move their hands. These are working women. Picking mussels or oysters from shells, they are telling local tales of mishaps and adventures, cakes burned, nets ripped and torn, the behaviour of local girls: Elsie, Hilda, Edna May, Phyllis and Florrie, who have I forgotten? Dolly and Gladys? Mary. You are the wives of fishermen. Soon you will rear children, too many to fit in one stone cottage. Your children will spill out upon the shore. This is where they will play. They will grow up with sand and salt beneath their nails. Pick oysters and mussels from shells, repair nets. Learn to shield their eyes from the sun.

The light is fading through the window – the painter's back aches – he lifts his palette knife, and the paint falls thickly over the circle of white. He can touch it now. White layers surfacing, rising, foaming waves. The artist knows we want to touch the infinite: the ephemeral silvery moon, the blue-purple-pink sunset. We want to hold it in our hands. That raised surface moving towards us, the invisible made visible, the marks of the knife left on the canvas: small delicate ridges, he pets them. Fingers, hands, muscle, bone, once moving, now feeling. The painter raises his fingers. He wants to touch it, to shape it, and so the edge of the knife is scraping against the canvas board, a silver blade circling around the harbour basin. The painter who stood on the far side of the harbour holds up his knife to the sun. He is a lonely creature; he stands beneath the louring sky waiting to see what will come.

'And I saw an angel standing in the sun, and she cried with a loud voice.'

His knife moves around the rim of the harbour basin. She

is flipping and flapping; he watches her circle and hover. There is the pencil, there is the knife, both carry the light. He carries the pencil in his pocket, his sketchbook under his arm, the artist surrounded by water. Water, paper, knife, pencil, but everywhere he sees the spinning knife, his blade, his thumb, they wheel and work. He scrapes away at the honeyed gum with his little finger. It burns. Hours pass, and his fingers are on fire, singed and torn. He forgets. His neck stoops, his shoulders crick. He forgets.

Nothing should seep too deep; the red and blue must meet with the white and gold. His finger spirals and turns, a small brush clenched in his hand while his feet kick sideways. Two phials of dark water run over his shoes. The painter curses but he keeps moving, whipping his knife up towards the canvas. Now the moon is shining. He cricks his neck towards the window and nods. Just above his head, through the glass pane, she lands on his hand and spreads. Blurs watery light. He smiles and nods again, and his hand moves back and forth in rapid circles, light. His transparent paste of white and yellow is spreading, spreading out across the shore. Nothing must be still now; everything must dance upon the white wings of the bird. Wing, waves, white circles, they spread. And she is there, coming through the light, the woman, the girl, both waving.

'The artist is our only hope for we are all in the soup.'
(Mary Neal)

Acknowledgements

I HAVE many people to thank and a poor memory; the Goddess Mnemosyne is not always on my side; nowadays she seems to take frequent sabbaticals. However, I have had several Green Ladies in my life – guardian spirits – literary trustees.

I must thank my editor at William Collins, Arabella Pike, for continuing to support me and for trusting me to produce a book during difficult circumstances: the world before and after the pandemic which altered all of us. Thank you for your patience, kindness and loyalty.

Thank you to Helen Ellis at William Collins for your wit and grace and persistent support; for your shared love of gardens and flowers, an early language.

Thank you to Sarah Chalfant of the Wylie Agency for reading and responding so sensitively to drafts in written and audio form. Thank you for continuing to support my writing and for seeing what it is and what it is still becoming. The blood jet of poetry still flows. Thank you to Jessica Bullock too for your professional support and discretion and your kind communication, for your reassurance and attention, for your wisdom.

A special thank you to Alba Ziegler-Bailey whose ability to read and respond so intuitively I will miss hugely. Alba, you are a large part of this book, and I could hear your voice as I was editing. Your spirit was everywhere. You have been a great source of support and inspiration for me. A literary sister. Thank you so much.

Thank you to Lucy Neal, great great niece of Mary Neal who in 1993 handed Mary's papers to the Vaughan Williams Memorial Library. Thank you to Lucy and the Mary Neal online project for enabling me to discover Mary's story. This is an imagined biography – in fragments and parts – but without those preserved prompts I would not have been able to carry Mary's life into my own. Thank you to Mary for presiding so clearly and so firmly; your bright light still shines.

Thank you to Suzie Hanna and Bobby Hanna for their continued love and trust; thank you especially to Suzie for reading early drafts; some of your Norfolk Tales are here, Suzie, some of your folk, your Wheatfen, your mother's capacity for bringing in strangers and feeding them; your capacity for caring for the strays. Once a foster mother always a foster mother.

Thank you to Anne Griffiths for her delicate and sensitive lines, for your creative companionship, your careful eyes and your exquisite draughtsmanship. Your drawings are perfect.

Thank you too to Iain Hunt who saw this book through several sensitive phases and whose kind and thoughtful copy-editing made the book 'just so'. Thank you, Iain, for granting me a vision of the book just when I needed it. 'Just exactly the right person,' as my grandmother would say.

I completed this book after a serious and yet incomplete diagnosis. A special thanks to Will Self for holding my hand, so to speak, during a wobbly editorial moment in the back of a car on the way down to Sussex. Thank you for being glad for me when the green light was given.

Thank you also to my friendly chauffeurs, Stephen and Duncan; thank you for turning that journey into a Pickwick picnic. You were great friends.

Thank you to Aunty Liz for understanding that this is a book for those not afraid of what lies beyond, and that only the imagination can help us 'see to see', as Emily Dickinson says.

I have many friends who have supported me during this period of writing: Josephine Reynell, Sunetra Gupta, Nadia Hilliard, Neil Armstrong, Ray and Aouicha Hilliard, Laura Ashby, Julie Sutherland, Monika Class, Lucie Richter-Mahr, Marc Lafrance, Alexandra Lewis, Jacqueline Norton, Catherine Coldstream, Dennis Harrison, Una Eve, Matthew Redhead, Mimi Eve, Nasir Khan, Duncan Minshull, Beth Egan, Vera Busse, Tracy Brain, Violet Henderson, Lemn Sissay.

Thank you especially to Tom MacFaul for teaching me things and for telling me I could write. Sometimes you just need to be told things.

A good teacher is the force that through the green fuse can drive the flower. My tutors at St Andrews – Stephen Boyd, Jane Stabler, Barbara Murray, Mr Herbert, Robert Crawford – I still remember your passion and ire for your literary worlds. To be cross is also to be kind. Crossness is a precise editorial form. It stamps out pretension, it weeds out the upstart, so the flower can be seen.

Thank you to Don Paterson for your encouraging words. You were not cross, only kind.

A special thank you to Katherine Muskett and Pratima

Mitchell, aka Nanu, for reading late drafts and reassuring me that I had not lost my voice or my intention. Thank you to Charlie Lee Potter for her unwavering encouragement of my creative vision and for that long long journey to Sussex and back we made to make our podcast; you are one of the few friends who has seen my precise starting point, that grey granite house by the sea with no sea view. That stumbling man with a bottle in his hand.

A very big thank you to Emma Hagestadt for reading several drafts so devotedly and especially during the difficult final stages with such belief.

Thank you to Sarah Pethybridge for sharing her homes with me and her love of small posies on windowsills; for the Cornish sea and birds and for so many kind and sustaining gifts and visits. For her belief in the need to sustain culture and the reading brain; for her understanding of good sentences (see George Eliot).

Thank you to Alice Jolly for encouraging me to continue with my literary experiments; thank you for your company and kinship and for allowing me to draw close to your felt words too.

Thank you too to Rebecca Abrams whose belief in literature as a form of art sustains me: the power of literary experiment and voice. Italy! The sun! Intimate conversation working its own clarification. Thank you to Kate Clanchy whose strength, loyalty and nobility is enough to build a new Roman forum. You are a true empress.

Thank you to Marina Warner for your care and attention and literary friendship. I hope I can honour your tradition, what you have set down for us all to follow: your wisdom, your fables and fairy tales – you made them your own – your familial stories, your great belief and hope in the arts and the intellectual imagination. Your cultural curatorship to which we are all indebted.

A special thank you to my friend Maeve Magnus (age 7, going on wise) who is always marvellous and has been a true friend; thank you for making me laugh so hard I had to lie on the floor. You have taught me that the recovery position is always through laughter. Thank you to Tom and Outi for trusting me with her and thank you for your neighbourly care; thank you Outi for sharing a love of words with me. Thank you to all my neighbours on Rope Ham Island for whom green things are the basic source of life. We are surrounded by them; we notice them; we tend to them.

A special thanks to Will May and Andrew Blades for listening to several parts. At some point the words must be spoken; they must dance. Thank you too to Andrea Macrae for your literary kinship and precise and sensitive mind, your way of seeing. Thank you also to Andrew Smith for celebrating the oral tradition from which this book emerges and for allowing me to record with you. Our podcasts have been a great source of joy and playful inspiration.

Thank you to my family in Mallorca, Catalina and Richard, Alba and Soraya; the figure of Mary Neal came to me some years ago now – one Mallorcan Christmas – by your fire. I expect it was the influence of my feminist-suffragist sister, Catalina, who summoned her from the flames.

Thank you to my parents, Rosemary and Eric Thompson and my sister, Susie, and my brother, Richard. And to my other brothers, Daniel, Jamie and John. Thank you to Grace Ottmann for always being there; your spirit continues, and I sense it always will because you are another Mary.

And most of all thank you to my grandmother, Edna May Turner, for teaching me how to read the signs of the small and the invisible; for showing me what the weather might mean and the shape of a leaf in my hand. Never knock the plants, they have their lives too, and we all need watering. As a child you set my roots down, you watered me, and I grew. Thank you for your love and attention, which in its highest form is a kind of prayer (Simone Weil).